MAKING FREUD
MORE FREUDIAN

MAKING FREUD MORE FREUDIAN

Arnold Rothstein

KARNAC

First published in 2010 by
Karnac Books Ltd
118 Finchley Road, London NW3 5HT

British Library Cataloguing in Publication Data

A C.I.P. for this book is available from the British Library

ISBN: 978 1 85575 731 8

Edited, designed and produced by The Studio Publishing Services Ltd
www.publishingservicesuk.co.uk
e-mail: studio@publishingservicesuk.co.uk

www.karnacbooks.com

CONTENTS

ABOUT THE AUTHOR

Dr Rothstein practises psychoanalysis in New York City. He teaches psychoanalytic theory and technique at the New York Psycho-analytic Institute and the Institute for Psychoanalytic Education, affiliated with NYU School of Medicine. He is currently Program Chair for North America of the International Psychoanalytical Association.

Dr Rothstein has authored numerous papers, as well as three books: *The Narcissistic Pursuit of Perfection*, *The Structural Hypothesis: An Evolutionary Perspective*, and *Psychoanalytic Technique and the Creation of Psychoanalytic Patients*. He has also edited seven books, and is the founding editor of the Workshop Series of the American Psychoanalytic Association.

Dr Rothstein completed training in psychoanalysis at the Columbia Psychoanalytic Center for Training and Research in 1971 and was on its faculty until 1988. He established the Mental Health Department at the Lexington School for the Deaf in 1971 and was its Medical Director until 1984. Dr Rothstein was also Director of Training in Psychotherapy at St. Luke's Hospital in New York City from 1980 to 1988, as well as Chair of the Program Committee of the American Psychoanalytic Association from 1990 to 1996.

Introduction

The purpose of this book is to demonstrate the clinical value of the theoretical contributions of Charles Brenner. For more than half a century, Brenner worked to make Freud more Freudian by selectively elaborating what is of enduring value in Freud's writings and by discarding what is misguided in it. Brenner's edifice is built on an elaboration of Arlow's (1969) concept "fantasy function" and Freud's (1894) concept "compromise formation".

For Freud, the concept "compromise formation" usually refers to two psychic elements, a drive and defence, combining to result in a symptom. Brenner elaborated the concept to describe the dynamic organization of complexes of interacting unconscious fantasies each created by the influences of drive derivatives (wishes), affects (anxiety and depressive affect), defences, and the contributions of conscience.

In *Structural Hypothesis: An Evolutionary Perspective*, I (1983) distinguished between revolutionary and evolutionary perspectives on the development of psychoanalytic theories. I stated,

> A revolutionary perspective, such as that proposed by Schafer (1976) or Kohut (1977), views paradigms as relatively static

> constructs and proposes to divest psychoanalysis of old models and
> to substitute entirely new theories in their place. An evolutionary
> perspective strives to accommodate (in the Piagetian sense) the
> traditional model to novelty and new data. [p. 1]

In 1983, Brenner's contributions could be understood as evolutionary elaborations of Freud's structural hypothesis. In 1994,
Brenner discarded the structural hypothesis because he found its
organizing constructs, id, ego, and superego, imprecise and misleading. Brenner's 1994 contribution seemed revolutionary, yet he
maintained the essential elements of Freud's model while divesting
it of its obfuscating jargon. I experience this elaboration as more
than evolutionary and yet not quite revolutionary in the Kuhnian
(1962) sense of the term.

Subsequent to 1994, Brenner can be characterized as a "modernist". A modernist, according to the art historian, Varnedoe (1990),
is someone who breaks new ground without abandoning tradition.
(I am indebted to Dr Claudia Lament for introducing me to Dr
Varnedoe's ideas. I owe my characterization of them to her.) The
new is created from the elements of the established paradigm but
in a surprising way by re-thinking them and presenting them in a
new and more clinically useful way. The contributions of the last
fourteen years of Brenner's life are in the modernist tradition.

Brenner's (1982, 1994, 1998, 2002) theoretical contributions are
presented almost devoid of clinical data. The purpose of this book
is to provide data that are intended to demonstrate the clinical
value of Brenner's theoretical proposals.

Chapter One delineates what is of enduring value in Freud's
writings as well as elements of his work that, paradoxically, *may*
be employed in the service of resistance to appreciating the ubiquitous and interminable influence of unconscious conflict on all
human thought and activity. In addition, the post Freudian process
of divesting Freud of its anti-Freudian aspects is described.

The subsequent chapters discuss specific subjects. These discussions are explicated with detailed analytic data.

In Chapter Two, narcissism is defined as a fantasy of perfection
best understood as a compromise formation. In Chapter Three,
masochistic fantasies and enactments are explored from the organizing perspective of compromise formation theory. In Chapter

Four, shame and guilt are understood as affects with similar fantasies contents, again best understood as compromise formations. The three chapters, as a unit, demonstrate the common interrelationships between narcissism, masochism, and sadism. They demonstrate that masochistic and sadistic phenomena are, in my experience, always welded to narcissistic fantasies. This relationship seems so ubiquitous that, in addition to the term sadomasochism, it is worth considering the terms sado-narcissism and maso-narcissism.

Chapters Five though Seven present analytic data related to specific clinical topics in which the work was conducted from the organizing perspective of compromise formation theory. Chapter Five describes analytic work with a patient who wanted to give the analyst a large sum of money.

Chapter Six explores the clinical advantages of considering patients' reluctances to one or another of the parameters of the analytic situation as motivated by complexes of unconscious fantasies.

Chapter Seven distinguishes psychiatric and psychoanalytic diagnoses. The clinical advantages of conceiving psychoanalytic diagnoses as co-created fantasies are explored.

Chapter Eight delineates the failure of the paradigm for evaluating and selecting subjects, considered analysable, for psychoanalytic therapy. An alternative "trusting" model is described emphasizing analytic attitude and the interminability of the analyst's subjectivity.

Finally, the conclusion emphasizes that the ideas of the "fantasy function" of the mind and of the ubiquity of unconscious conflict requires that all psychoanalytic theories be understood to conceive of all perceptions as subjective and of all relationships as intersubjective.

PART I
THEORETICAL CONSIDERATIONS

Making Freud more Freudian: a reading

T he premise of this chapter is that there has existed an implicit purpose in an aspect of post-Freudian psychoanalytic psychology: that of making Freud more Freudian. I will make that trend explicit, first by outlining essential tenets of Freud's seminal contributions. Then I describe aspects of Freud's writings that may be confusing, may obfuscate, and/or may be employed in the service of defending against assimilating essential Freudian constructs. Finally, I delineate aspects of the contributions of Jacob Arlow, Charles Brenner, and others who have contributed to the process of making Freud more Freudian. These contributors selectively elaborated what is of enduring value in Freud's writings and discarding what is misguided in it.

Fundamental Freudian premises

Freud's (1900a) most important postulate was his description of unconscious motivation. He (1900a, 1905a, 1923) delineated the nature of motivation as sexual and outlined its development beginning in the earliest days of life. Emphasizing the oedipal phase as a particularly important organizer of children's conflicted infantile sexual wishes (1923), he (1901) stressed that conflicted infantile sexual wishes *may* influence seemingly unrelated everyday adult functioning.

Freud's earliest model was based on an insight that stressed the pursuit of forbidden sexual pleasure. However, clinical experience impressed him with the complexity of manifest motivation. He (1916) described "exceptions" (p. 311) who felt entitled to pursue vengeance, as well as people who were "criminals from a sense of guilt" (p. 332) or were "wrecked by success" (p. 316). These clinical experiences led him to write theoretical papers in an attempt to explain narcissism (1914a) and masochism (1916), and to broaden his concept of defence (1915a).

1920 was a watershed year for Freud. He revised his instinct theory, placing aggressive wishes on a par with sexual wishes. Relatedly (1900a, 1920), he revised his dream theory, distinguishing an unconscious wish for punishment from an unconscious wish for sexual pleasure, and placing the former on an equal level with infantile sexual wishes. In elaborating these complexities, Freud was, in part, making his model more psychological, and, therefore, more Freudian.

In 1923 and 1926, Freud proposed his final revised model of the mind. In his first model, only infantile sexual wishes are unconscious. In his final model, the concept of unconscious is redefined and broadened. Aggressive, as well as sexual, wishes are unconscious and conceived of as the "id". Defences are an unconscious function of the ego, and guilt—understood as the unconscious wish (fear) for (of) punishment—is attributed to the superego. As part of this major revision, Freud (1926) discarded his first biologically-conceived affect theory and replaced it with a psychological signal theory of anxiety. Finally, Freud proposed a theory of technique that provides analysts with a method for being with, listening to, and understanding another person.

This brief summary emphasizes that Freud's contributions remain the foundation of a contemporary psychoanalytic psychology. However, paradoxically, there are three areas of his theoretical writings that are anti-Freudian, that is, they may be employed to deny the ubiquity and centrality of conflict and, relatedly, the organizing centrality of the pleasure principle in mental life. These three areas are Freud's: (1) biological theories of motivation; (2) distinctions between the pleasure principle and the reality principle (1911); (3) the concept of motivation that is "beyond the pleasure principle" (1920).

Anti-Freudian hypotheses

Freud's emphasis on the biological basis of motivation is evident from his earliest (1895a) to his final (1937) statements. He (1937) stated, "for the psychical field, the biological field does in fact play the part of the underlying bedrock" (p. 252). This emphasis influenced his psychological conceptions.

In the *Project for a Scientific Psychology*, Freud's biological orientation is explicit. He (1895a) stated that the aim of this project "is to represent psychical processes as quantitatively determined data of specifiable material particles" (p. 355). He continued, "it is to be assumed that the material particles in question are the neurons . . . [the] process of discharge [of quantity] is the primary function of neuronic systems" (pp. 355–357).

The shadow of the "Project" can be seen in derivative metaphors in later theoretical works. I conjecture that one of its functions was to provide Freud with convenient biological explanations for his failures. It helped him avoid considering the possibility that his pessimism was a response to the limits of his psychological understanding. In "Analysis terminable and interminable", Freud (1937) explained his failures as the result, in part, of "a constitutional strength of instinct [which made them] . . . recalcitrant to taming by the ego" (p. 220). Freud proposed that certain people suffer from "adhesiveness of the libido [and added that] . . . we can discover no special reason for this cathectic loyalty" (*ibid.*, p. 249).

In the same paper, his discussion of negative therapeutic reaction demonstrated the simultaneous existence of his psychological and quasi-biological theories of motivation. Freud (1937) proposed that negative therapeutic reaction is due to "the sense of guilt and the need for punishment" (p. 242). He proceeded to qualify his clinical explanation by adding,

> But this is only one portion of it which is, as it were, psychically bound by the superego and thus becomes recognizable; other

quotas of the same force . . . may be at work in other, unspecified places . . . these phenomena are unmistakable indicators of the presence of . . . the death instinct. [p. 242–245]

Maintaining a purely psychological perspective with patients in such negative states of mind requires that analysts tolerate the unpleasure evoked in them over many years, while simultaneously assimilating the inevitable limits of their understanding.

The terms "libido" and "destrudo" were Freud's metaphors for the material particles he fantasized to exist in neurons. Freud was *intellectually* aware of the speculative nature of his instinct theory. In *The Ego and the Id* (1923), he stated, "the distinction between two classes of instincts does not seem sufficiently assured, and it is possible that the facts of clinical analysis may be found which will do away with its pretension" (p. 42). Nevertheless, Freud (*ibid.*) repetitively relied on the idea of "instinctual defusion" of the life (eros) and death (thanatos) instincts to explain the limits of the therapeutic efficacy of his psychoanalytic technique. Freud (*ibid.*) stated, "instinctual defusion and the marked emergence of the death instinct call for particular consideration among the effects of some severe neuroses—for instance, the obsessional neuroses". Finally, one of Freud's elaborations of his instinct theory may be employed to contribute to the illusion that there exists an area of mental functioning beyond conflict. In *The Ego and the Id*, Freud (1923) suggested that sublimation "implied an abandonment of sexual aims, a desexualization" (p. 30). Hartmann's (1939) elaboration of the idea of "autonomous" mental functioning can be understood as an extension of this resistant conceptualization.

In formulating "two principles of mental functioning", Freud (1911, p. 218) distinguished neurotic thinking from normal thinking. Freud (*ibid.*) experienced "the neurotic turning away from reality because they find it unbearable". He conceived of neurotics' thinking as similar to that of very young children. He characterized this thinking as "primary process" (*ibid.*, p. 219) thinking, governed by the "pleasure principle [whose] processes strive towards gaining pleasure" (*ibid.*). By contrast, the "*reality principle*" (*ibid.*) characterizes mature adult thinking, including "*attention . . . notation . . .* [and] *memory*" functions of the mind which allowed for "*an impartial passing of judgement,* which had to decide whether the given idea is true or false" (*ibid.*, p. 221).

Freud's belief in the capacity of the human mind to make impartial judgements and to distinguish between what is true and what is false facilitates the illusion of a capacity for objectivity. Belief in the analyst's capacity for objectivity has been attractive to many colleagues. It resonates with the illusionary ideas that conflicts can be worked through and resolved, and that there is an area of mental functioning that is beyond conflict. Hartmann (1939) elaborated this ideal conception of "a conflict free" (p. 3) sphere of mental functioning. These illusions are in marked contrast to what I suggest is a more contemporary Freudian conception of the ubiquity of subjectivity and the interminable nature of conflict. Conflicts are worked on interminably, and are never fully or completely resolved.

In 1920, Freud distinguished pathology that derived from trauma from pathology that is derived from neurotic conflict. He conceived of a traumatized person as someone who experiences a "*passive* situation" (1920, p. 16). The subject is then compelled to repeat that situation to gain the illusion of "*active*" (*ibid.*) control of it. Freud (1920) proposed that "the compulsion to repeat overrides the pleasure principle" (p. 22). Finally, Freud understood the compulsion to repeat to derive from very early attempts to master anxiety. He described his eighteen-month-old nephew's attempts to master separation as an example of such an attempt at mastery (*ibid.*, pp. 14–15).

Freud's distinction between a traumatized mind and a conflicted mind has been employed by relational schools to emphasize the organizing impact of preoedipal rather than oedipal development. Such theorists highlight the quality of the nurturing parent rather than conflicted infantile sexual development in the genesis of human suffering. Freud's distinction between the compulsion to repeat and the pleasure principle facilitates this either/or kind of thinking.

Making Freud more Freudian

The main tactic that certain post Freudian American analysts employed in making Freud more Freudian has been to debiologize Freudian theory. They have done so by differentiating Freud's biologically-based instinct theory from his more clinically-based theory. The latter emphasizes clinical data related to what Arlow (1969) termed the "fantasy function" of the mind.

Analytic failures are often characterized by their recalcitrant masochistic features. To explain his failures, Freud frequently resorted to experience-distant biological conceptions. Prior to 1920, masochism was conceived as secondary phenomena to sadism. In 1920, Freud tentatively suggested that "there *might* be such a thing as primary masochism" (1920, p. 55). By 1924, Freud was more definitive in his conception of a primary masochism derived from the death instinct. He stated, "Erotogenic masochism accompanies the libido through all its developmental phases and derives from them its changing psychical coatings" (1924, pp. 164–165).

In 1955, in a panel on masochism, Arlow provided a framework for debiologizing Freud. He asserted: "such biological speculations are undesirable in the context of clinical discussions, since they involve extrapolations which are incapable of confirmation or contradiction in [the analytic] setting" (Stein, 1956, p. 526).

Four years later, Brenner considered the masochistic character from the clinical perspective that Arlow had emphasized. Brenner conceived of masochism as within the pleasure principle and as a legacy of the Oedipal phase of development. In reviewing the literature on masochism, Brenner presaged his later emphasis on the construct compromise formation. Although all contributions to the subject stressed the over-determination of masochism, most presented unifactorial emphases. Many contributors emphasized the importance of the traumatic nature of pre-Oedipal object relations and of an ego functioning "beyond the pleasure principle".

In their 1964 book, Arlow and Brenner continued their effort to make Freud more Freudian by helping analysts mourn their investments in his topographic theory and mine the advantages of the structural theory. They emphasized the importance of Freud's concept "compromise formation". They stated,

> Within the framework of the topographic theory this idea occupies an important position, but a somewhat limited one . . . within the framework of the structural theory, however, the ideas of a multiplicity of causal [psychological] factors play a much larger role . . . every thought, every mental act is the result of a compromise or

interaction among the various functions of the mind, i.e., among id, superego, and ego. [pp. 47–48]

Arlow's purpose in his classic 1969 paper was to place the concept of unconscious fantasy squarely within the organizing framework of the structural hypothesis. Arlow stated that the "unconscious fantasy function" (p. 158) and the "fantasy activity [it generates] is a *constant* feature of mental life" (p. 159). Arlow added:

> unconscious fantasy activity provides the mental set in which sensory stimuli are perceived and integrated [and] . . . It is this activity that supplies the mental set in which the data of perception are organized, judged and interpreted. [pp. 161, 173]

Arlow's 1969 paper has revolutionary implications for the development of Freudian theory. If all perception is constantly influenced by the unconscious fantasy function of the mind, then Freud's conception of the reality principle and the associated concept of objectivity are obviated. All perceptions are inevitably subjective. Subjectivity and, relatedly, intersubjectivity are ubiquitous characteristics of mental life.

In 1982, Brenner published *The Mind in Conflict*. This work built upon half a dozen papers he had written in the previous dozen years (1968, 1974, 1975, 1979a,b, 1980). The book represents Brenner's final attempt to work within the organizing framework of the structural hypothesis. *The Mind in Conflict* makes Freud more Freudian by clarifying and elaborating his fundamental organizing concepts: drive, affect, defence, conflict, compromise, and the organizing importance of the Oedipal phase of development.

Brenner distinguished libidinal and aggressive drives as generalizations from the concept drive derivative. He stated: "A drive derivative is a wish for gratification . . . [it] is unique, individual and specific" (1982, p. 26). Brenner stressed that "Drive derivatives are substantially influenced by experience, especially with respect to aims and object" (p. 39).

Brenner reminded us that *"ideas and sensations together constitute an affect* as a psychological phenomena [and stressed that] whatever the affect . . . the ideas, [the sensations], or both may be wholly or partially unconscious or otherwise warded off" (*ibid.*, p. 41).

Brenner then differentiated between anxiety and depressive affect based on a temporal distinction. "Anxiety is [the sensation of] unpleasure plus a particular set of ideas [that] something unpleasurable is going to happen" (*ibid.*, p. 43). Depressive affect is the sensation of unpleasure "associated with ideas of a calamity that has already happened" (*ibid.*, p. 47).

Brenner stressed the triggering relationship between affects and conflict. Conflict occurs whenever a drive derivative and/or superego demand and/or prohibition arouses anxiety or depressive affect.

The concept of depressive affect is, perhaps, Brenner's most original contribution. In elaborating Freud's (1926) signal anxiety theory, Brenner provided a dynamic context for clinical phenomena referred to as disorders of self-esteem and counters the tendency to treat depressive phenomena as diagnosable diseases.

Brenner revised the concept of defence by broadening it and defining it "only in terms of its consequence: the reduction of anxiety and/or depressive affect associated with drive derivative or with superego functioning" (1982, p. 73) [and] "whatever . . . results in a diminution of anxiety or depressive affect belongs under the heading of defense" (*ibid.*, p. 72). Brenner's broadening of the concept of defence emphasized that no defence is limited to a particular type of conflict or patient. His revision rendered the more limited concept of defence mechanism obsolete. In describing the concept depressive affect (1975, 1979a) Brenner elaborated Freud's danger situations to be subsequently understood as "the calamities of childhood" (1982, p. 83). In discussing the calamities Brenner emphasized "that the three calamities . . . are always intimately . . . interwoven" (*ibid.*, p. 94). He stressed that

> Rivalrous incestuous and parenticidal drive derivative have, as part of their content, thoughts of object loss ("Death wishes") and loss of love ("fantasies of punishment and retribution") as well as thoughts of castration . . . in every individual all three calamities participate in the anxiety and depressive affect that initiate conflict in the oedipal period. [*ibid.*, p. 107]

In discussing the concept compromise formation, Brenner, once again, broadened Freud's conception. Brenner emphasized that

Freud conceived of drive derivatives reaching consciousness as the result of failure of repression. Brenner defined "compromise formations [as] a general tendency of the mind, not an exceptional one" (1982, p. 113). Brenner proposed that "the entire range of psychic phenomena" (*ibid.*, p. 109) is understood to derive from psychic conflict the components of which are "drive derivatives, anxiety and/or depressive affect and defense" (*ibid.*).

In discussing the superego, Brenner proposed that "the superego is both a consequence of psychic conflict and a component of it" (*ibid.*, p. 120). At this point in the development of his thinking, Brenner needed to conceive of the superego as "both" in order to maintain his fealty to Freud's structural hypothesis. However, his italicized definition of the superego heralds his future discarding of the term. Brenner stated *"the superego is a compromise formation, to be more precise, a group of compromise formations originating largely in the oedipal phase"* (*ibid.*). For Brenner, the superego is a dynamic complex of fantasies, not a structure. Defining the superego as a complex of compromise formations allowed Brenner to explain its functioning as "defense at one time, the equivalent of a drive derivative arousing unpleasure at another time, and a calamitous unpleasure to be [defended against] at still another" (*ibid.*, p. 121).

The concept compromise formation allowed Brenner to define pathology and distinguish it from normality in a clearly psychoanalytic manner. His diagnostic schema diminishes the tendency to conflate psychoanalytic and psychiatric perspectives. Brenner stated,

> a compromise formation is pathological when it is characterized by any combination of the following features: too much restriction of gratification of drive derivatives, too much inhibition of functional capacity, too much unpleasure . . . too great a tendency to injure or destroy oneself, or too great conflict with one's environment. [*ibid.*, p. 150]

Brenner's 1982 book, *The Mind In Conflict*, heralded his 1994 paper in which he suggested maintaining the core clinical elements of conflict, drive, unpleasure, and defence, while relinquishing the terms id, ego, and superego. Brenner's clinical experience convinced him that there is no

structure or agency of the mind, the id, that consists of drive derivatives; [no] separate . . . agency of the mind, the ego, which has
other functions, including defense; and that both are separate from
still another structure the superego. [p. 479]

Brenner emphasized that the idea of an ego that objectively accesses
external reality has particular disadvantages. Deriving from
Arlow's (1969) proposal that "every perception gratifies one or more
drive derivatives, in however disguised a way", Brenner stated,

> There is no specified rational part of the mind that takes realistic
> account of external reality without being motivated by the libidinal
> and aggressive wishes of childhood and the unpleasure associated
> with those wishes. [1994, p 478]

Once again, it is noteworthy that this perspective stressed the ubiquity of subjectivity. In a number of papers over the next fourteen
years, Brenner (1998, 2000, 2002) reiterated and elaborated his jour-
ney "beyond the ego and the id".

In his final paper, Brenner (2008) stressed the importance of
drive theory by delineating and clarifying distinctions between
biological speculations about motivations from conceptions more
closely related to psychoanalytically-informed observations. Brenner provides a drive theory that is not only clear, but also "user
friendly", in current jargon.

Brenner emphasized that Freud never clearly and fully outlined
a theory of motivation. In discussing that paper I (2008) emphasized that this obfuscation is, in part, the result of Freud's tendency
to conceive of drive theory on two complementary levels of abstrac-
tion: the biological and the psychological. Experience-distant
concepts "eros" and "thanatos", generating libido and destrudo,
complement the clinically available idea that Freud (1900a) clearly
stated in Chapter Seven of *The Interpretation of Dreams:* "Dreams are
nothing more than the fulfilment of wishes" (p. 550) [and] *"a wish
that is represented in a dream must be an infantile one"* (p. 553). In his
effort to emphasize that the infantile sexual wishes influencing
human behaviour are "anything but stereotyped", Brenner distinguished between the German terms *Trieb* and *Instinkt.* In doing so,
he stressed what he stated in 1982: "a wish . . . has personal history,
a uniquely personal form, and a uniquely personal content" (p. 22).

Brenner (2008) proceeded to critique Freud's biological drive theory in order to delineate his own version of a clinical drive theory. I take a slightly different approach in reading Freud's drive theories. I believe that Brenner is correct in viewing Freud's biological drive theory as invalid. However, Freud's clinical drive theory is quite close to Brenner's own improved elaboration of Freud's clinical proposition. Both stressed the fundamental importance of infantile sexual wishes organized in the Oedipal stage of development. Brenner added an emphasis upon the ubiquity and interminability of conflict related to these wishes. This emphasis on the relationship of complex wishes in the functioning of conscience, and the related concept "depressive affect", are important elaborations of Freud's clinical drive theory.

Brenner (2008) suggested that the question, "why [Freud] clung to the idea [mind and body] are separable . . . is a question that will never be satisfactorily answered" (p. 5). I agree. I would add that Freud clung to his related biological drive theory. I do not have Freud on my couch, but I will speculate about Freud's motives.

I conjecture that Freud inevitably needed his biological drive theory for subjective, personal reasons. In *Civilization and Its Discontents* (1930), Freud stated,

> The assumptions of the existence of an instinct of death . . . has met with resistance even in analytic circles . . . To begin with [in *Beyond the Pleasure Principle*] it was only tentatively that I put forward the views I have developed here, but in the course of time they have gained such a hold on me that I can no longer think in any other way. [p. 119]

I hypothesize that Freud needed to feel he was a physician and scientist. Being just a psychoanalytic psychologist was probably not enough for him. It seems to me that many colleagues have similar narcissistic conflicts in accepting that they are psychoanalysts rather than psychiatrists. In addition, I suggest that Freud could employ his biological drive theory to avoid the narcissistic injury of assimilating the limits of the therapeutic efficacy of *his* psychoanalytic technique. Freud acknowledged his narcissistic vulnerability in response to Binswanger, stating, "The eye that sees cannot see itself".

Thus, Brenner (2008) proceeded to make explicit what is implicit in Freud's clinical drive theory. The pleasure-seeking wishes of childhood are always incestuous and murderous and, I would add, always bisexual. Brenner (2008) stressed that these wishes are "associated . . . as closely with unpleasure as with pleasure . . . Defense against pleasure-seeking wishes is as much a part of the mind as is the striving for pleasure" (p. 10). Brenner correctly emphasized that the "significant practical importance" of his contribution is that it helps the analyst to avoid unifactorial interpretations and to remember that "aggressive wishes are just as sexual as libidinal ones" (p. 10). Charles Brenner's contributions help the analyst to keep analysing, as the mind is interminably in conflict.

I conclude my consideration of the contributions of Jacob Arlow and Charles Brenner by reiterating that by making Freud more Freudian, they contributed to the possibility that the eye that sees will momentarily see itself more clearly.

The 1950s witnessed a focused interest in the subject of masochism. The period 1966 to 1977 was characterized by a similar intense interest in narcissism and difficult patients "diagnosed" "narcissistic" and/or "borderline". Kohut and Kernberg were the main contributors to these considerations. Kohut (1966, 1968, 1971) emphasized failures in very early maternal responsiveness in the genesis of fixations in the development of narcissistic libido, resulting in patients labelled with narcissistic personality disorders. Kohut considered borderline patients to be latent schizophrenics. Kernberg (1967, 1970, 1975) described a pre-Oedipal fixation expressed with a Kleinian emphasis on aggression and splitting. He diagnosed patients afflicted with this fixation as "borderline personalities", and considered "narcissistic personalities" to be a variety of the former state.

I was a candidate at Columbia University Psychoanalytic Clinic at that time. When these difficult patients were discussed, it was always considered a question of whether Kohut's or Kernberg's contributions were more helpful in attempting to work with such analysands. I remember thinking that it seemed odd that Freud's ideas were not seriously considered in these discussions. Then I remembered Hartmann's comment concerning narcissism in his paper on the ego. He noted that

Many analysts do not find it altogether easy to define the place
which the concept of narcissism holds in present analytic theory.
This, I think, is mainly due to the fact that this concept has not been
explicitly redefined in terms of Freud's later structural psychology.
[1950, p. 83]

During the 1970s, I wrote a number of papers (1977, 1979a,b),
culminating in my 1980 book *The Narcissistic Pursuit of Perfection*,
the explicit purpose of which was to define narcissism within the
structural hypothesis. I suggest the work also contributed to
making Freud more Freudian. Studying Freud's "introduction" to
the subject of narcissism (1914a, p. 6) led to the awareness that clarification of the concept, rather than redefinition, was required. As
with all of Freud's important theoretical considerations, he proposed two complementary theoretical explanations: an experience-
distant instinctual definition of narcissism as a component of
instinct theory (i.e., as narcissistic libido), and a clinically "close"
definition as a fantasy of "perfection" (p. 84). I (1980) proposed that
the term *narcissism* be defined in the latter manner, as a fantasy of
perfection. The phrase "fantasy of perfection" is employed as a
generalization. Fantasies of perfection are expressed in ideas of
omniscience or omnipotence. A subject or object is thought of as
most knowing, most powerful, most beautiful, most successful.
What is common to all is a superlative designation, such as "most",
and the absolute quality of this designation. Fantasies of perfection
are also associated with the number "one", and often with the wish
to be the "one and only". Fantasies of perfection are a ubiquitous
aspect of human experience that lead to distortion of one's sense of
reality, particularly as this relates to one's sense of vulnerability and
finiteness.

   In the decade following the publication of my 1980 book, and in
response to Brenner's *The Mind in Conflict*, in which narcissism is
rarely mentioned, I published a paper (1991) that correlated Freud's
clinical definition of narcissism as a fantasy of perfection with
Brenner's elaboration of the concept compromise formation. A
limited definition of the term *narcissism* as a fantasy of perfection
allows for a conception of narcissism as a compromise formation. Like all compromise formations, a fantasy of perfection is
composed of interacting drive derivatives, unpleasurable affects,

defences, and superego elements. Because analysis of a fantasy of perfection typically reveals a series of related fantasies, in every case one finds in the underlying conflicts many different drive derivatives, many fears and miseries, many defences, and many of the influences of conscience.

Conceptualizing fantasies of perfection as compromise formations leads to a number of clinically valuable generalizations. First, fantasies of perfection have a development that is influenced, in part, by the development of calamities of childhood. Second, fantasies of perfection may function as defences to diminish the unpleasure that is characteristic of the calamities and conflict. From this perspective, a fantasy of perfection is one component of additional, more complex compromise formations. Third, the threat of the loss of a fantasy of perfection evokes anxiety, while the sense that the loss has occurred is associated with the experience of depressive affect.

Fantasies of perfection develop in synchrony with the child's ideas of the imagined calamities of childhood, and are employed to diminish the unpleasure that characterizes these calamities. For example, when a subject experiences unpleasure associated with the sense that love will be or is lost, fantasies of undoing the calamity may be associated with a sense that the subject is perfect and, therefore, lovable. Analogously, when castration is threatened, or is imagined to have actually occurred, subjects may attempt to undo the sense of calamity by imagining they have a penis (Rado, 1933) or by imagining they can seduce (Loewenstein, 1957) or defeat the castrator. Similar fantasies characterize aspects of the child's masochistic and narcissistic (Rothstein, 1984) responses to the calamity of imminent punishment.

As with the calamities of childhood, once the Oedipal epoch occurs, all the calamities and associated fantasies of perfection are usually so interwoven as to be virtually inseparable. Fantasies of perfection are important aspects of the compromise formations that constitute the subjects' consciences. The origins of the subject's ideals probably begin in the second year of life. However, once the child enters the Oedipal phase of life, living up to his ideals and winning his parents' approval are inevitably linked to conflicts concerning the sexual and murderous wishes that characterize that epoch.

Finally, conceiving of narcissism as a fantasy of perfection facil- itates an understanding of experiences considered "traumatic" and, relatedly, of the "repetition compulsion" within the pleasure prin- ciple. The repetition of traumatic situations—when associated with an illusion of active mastery—gratifies an unconscious fantasy of restoring a sense of perfection to one's sense of self.

Piers and Singer (1953) wrote an influential book in which they fundamentally distinguished between the affects of shame and guilt. They conceived of shame as a pre-Oedipal fixation in ego- ideal development. Guilt was understood to be related to later Oedipal conflicts and related superego functioning. Kohut (1977) and two of his followers, Broucek (1982) and Morrison (1984) elab- orated a traumatogenic conception of the genesis of shame. They propose that shame be considered the central organizing affect of the psychology of the self. Kohut (1977) proposed that shame triggered disturbances in patients suffering from narcissistic per- sonality disorders, while guilt triggered Oedipal conflicts in patients suffering from neuroses. In addition, he suggested that if children experienced optimal empathic nurturance in the pre- Oedipal phase, they would be insulated from disturbances of subsequent developmental phases.

As a corrective to this either/or mode of thinking, and in elab- oration of Brenner's (1982) conception of the superego as a set of compromise formations, I (1994) proposed that shame and guilt are affects with similar fantasized contents, that is, the calamity of parental disapproval and the striving to win or regain parental approval and love. All human beings have the potential to experi- ence shame and guilt. In addition to hypothesized inherited poten- tials that are beyond analytic validation, selected subjects who are particularly shame-prone have had shaping experiences with parents who enjoyed shaming or humiliating them. In this regard, I noted that selected narcissistic personality disorders

> were repeatedly humiliated by their parents as children. Humi- liation was more likely to occur when they failed to live up to their parents' narcissistically-invested fantasies for them or when their existence challenged their parents' other narcissistically-invested pursuits. In addition, they were exposed to their parents' more general penchant for humiliating those who failed them. [1984, p. 99]

In 1994, I emphasized that guilt, shame, humiliation, mortification, and remorse are conceived of as components of superego compromise formations. All these affects express ways people felt and/or fear disapproval. Shame expresses a fantasy of a particular kind of parental disapproval or loss of love, a punishment that is feared or is sensed to have occurred. When the punishment is feared, shame is anticipated and associated with anxiety, the specific ideational content of which depicts the particular manner in which subjects fear being shamed. When the punishment is felt to have occurred, the sense of shame is associated with depressive affect involving the ideational expression of the manner in which subjects feel they have been shamed. Subjects whose lives are dominated by shame depressive affect are often afflicted with disorders of self-esteem. In both shame anxiety and shame depressive affect, the content of the affect is shaped, in part, by real experiences from previous stages of life.

In 1983, Abend, Porder, and Willick published a book that provided a corrective to Kernberg's popularized considerations of borderline patients. In their book, they described analytic work with borderline patients from an evolving Freudian perspective informed by Brenner's contributions. For example, in response to the emphasis on the pre-Oedipal genesis of such patients' problems, they wrote,

> Although the current psychoanalytic literature on the borderline patient places great etiological emphasis on the child and his caretaking person during the first two years of life, we found that our patients experienced significant trauma during the oedipal phase itself and frequently afterward as well. While we attempted to understand how significant preoedipal conflicts influenced their ego development and the nature of their object relations, we could not determine that these early conflicts were *more crucial* than the later ones of childhood in producing borderline pathology. [p. 241]

Finally, Boesky (1991, pp. 77–83) presents the "clinical examples of sublimations, enactments, and of identification to demonstrate the usefulness of [the theoretic concept] compromise formation as a method to better understand patients" (p. 78).

In conclusion, it is important to emphasize the evolving nature of Freudian theory. Knowledge from all disciplines, but particularly knowledge gained from analytic work with a broad spectrum of analysands, facilitates that evolution. The work cited in this paper helps the analyst to keep analysing as he works to maintain a neutral attitude toward the inevitably intersubjectively experienced data.

CHAPTER TWO

Narcissism

Narcissism refers to the panoply of fantasies of perfection that are a ubiquitous aspect of the creative activities of the mind. This chapter describes some relationships between fantasies of perfection and the calamities of childhood. The defensive function of fantasies of perfection in reducing the unpleasure, anxiety, and depressive affect that characterizes the calamities of childhood is stressed. From this perspective, a fantasy of perfection is a defensive component of a compromise formation. However, because these fantasies, like all fantasies, are best understood as compromise formations in every case, one finds an interaction of drive derivatives, unpleasurable affects, defence, and superego elements. In addition, analysis of a fantasy of perfection typically reveals a series of related fantasies composed of many different wishes, many fears and miseries, many defences, and many superego manifestations in the underlying conflict(s).

In pursuing the goal of this chapter, narcissism is further redefined within an evolving Freudian model of psychic conflict. My purpose in writing *The Narcissistic Pursuit of Perfection* (1980) was to redefine narcissism following Hartmann's (1950) suggestion that the concept narcissism "had not been explicitly redefined in terms of Freud's later structural psychology". The book is in the "evolutionary" tradition Hartmann exemplified (see Rothstein, 1983, pp. 9–28) for an elaboration of the conception of "evolutionary" *vs.* "revolutionary" process in the development of science in general and psychoanalysis in particular).

The impetus for writing this chapter derives from the study of Brenner's (1982) *The Mind in Conflict.* The definition of narcissism as a fantasy of perfection is correlated with Brenner's contemporary elaboration of Freud's (1923, 1926) structural model.

The chapter is organized as follows: first, the relevant hypotheses of *The Mind in Conflict* are summarized. Second, my previous suggestions concerning the definition of narcissism as a fantasy of perfection are outlined. Third, some relationships between fantasies of perfection and the calamities of childhood are described. Then analytic data are presented to demonstrate the value of these theoretical considerations.

The Mind in Conflict

Brenner's book emphasizes that conflict and "compromise formation [are] a general tendency of the mind, not an exceptional one" (1982, p. 113). The conception of fantasy and idea as compromise formation results in an understanding of wish, affect, and other aspects of the ego, as well as the superego, both as compromise formations and components of compromise formations.

Another emphasis of the book is Brenner's distinction between a theoretical conception of a phenomenon in very young children and the meanings of adult analytic data. Brenner stresses that the analytic method illuminates complexities of meaning:

> one must keep in mind the complexities involved if one is to follow the full range of the analytic material of any patient. One must be prepared to see evidence of misery alternating with terror, of terror breeding misery, of loss of love implying castration, of castration depressive affect leading to object loss, and of all the other combinations of the ideational content of the calamities of childhood that characterize psychic life in the Oedipal phase of development. It is only by being prepared for these complex interrelations that one

can hope to catch the evidence for each of them as it appears in a given patient's analytical material (*ibid.*, p. 108).

In regard to the components of conflict, Brenner distinguishes between libidinal and aggressive drives as generalizations and their expressions in an individual's drive derivatives or wishes. Of the latter, Brenner states, "there are both libidinal and aggressive elements in every wish" (*ibid.*, p. 22) and a wish "has a uniquely personal history . . . form . . . and content" (*ibid.*). He alludes to the contributions of the other agencies of the mind to the content of wishes when he states, "the aims of both the libidinal and aggressive drives are influenced by experiential factors reflected in ego development" (*ibid.*, p. 31). The complexities of the meanings of wishes are emphasized in his description of "Drive as defense against drive" (*ibid.*, p. 34). Brenner states, "In every reaction formation drive derivatives are in conflict with one another . . . because one is used defensively to ward off the other in order to eliminate or alleviate unpleasure" (*ibid.*).

In regard to affects, Brenner emphasizes that "Ideas and sensation together constitute an affect as a psychological phenomenon" (*ibid.*, p. 41). Brenner's distinction between depressive affect and anxiety based on the temporal content of the ideation is important, highly original, and particularly relevant to understanding experiences of fantasies of perfection. He defines anxiety as "unpleasure plus [the idea] something unpleasurable is going to happen" (*ibid.*, p. 45), while depressive affect is defined as "unpleasure . . . associated with ideas of a calamity that has already happened" (*ibid.*, p. 47). Brenner alludes to the conception of affect as compromise formation and as a component of conflict when he states: "Affects are related not only to the gratification and frustration of drive derivatives; they are also related to the maturation and development of ego and superego" (*ibid.*, p. 51).

He emphasizes a developmental perspective in his description of the development of the calamities of childhood.

As Freud (1926) pointed out, these calamities assume positions of importance in psychic life in sequence rather than all together. Object loss begins to play a role before loss of love, while castration begins to play its role later than either of the other two. For this reason, each calamity is sometimes considered to be phase-specific.

Object loss is considered to be specific to the oral phase, loss of love to the anal phase, and castration to the phallic phase. This schema has value if it is understood to apply *to the approximate stage of development at which each calamity first assumes importance*. However, it must be kept clearly in mind that once it has become important, each calamity remains so throughout the remainder of childhood and, indeed, in adult life as well. Nor is each calamity kept separate from its fellows. On the contrary, all three become and remain intimately related (p. 68, my italics).

Brenner's conception of depressive affect facilitates an appreciation of the typical "danger situations" as "calamities", while his elaboration of the superego places central emphasis on the organizing function of guilt. He states,

> guilt, by which Freud meant fear of punishment, is the last of the typical danger situations of childhood. It appears later in the course of development than the other three calamities of childhood—object loss, loss of love, and castration—and, in a sense, once it has developed, it subsumes them all. [1982, pp. 120–121]

> For a young child, morality means, essentially, feeling, thinking, and behaving in such a way as to avoid the calamity of being punished ... The crucial questions are, "What will win or forfeit parental approval?" and, "What will rouse or dissipate parental wrath?" [*ibid.*, p. 123]

Brenner stresses "that all superego compromise formations are ways in which a child tells its parents 'Approve of me!—'Love me!'" (*ibid.*, p. 137). One important way of winning approval "is to be remorseful—to promise to be good and never again to do what is bad" (*ibid.*). From this perspective, shame is understood to reflect a variety of guilt. In shame, an aspect of the content of a subject's guilt invokes the idea that parental disapproval is associated with the idea of being judged as bad and/or wanting in some quality or capacity. In addition, there may be a sense of being laughed at by the disapproving parent. In "Fear of humiliation" (Rothstein, 1984), I noted that the patients I was describing "were repeatedly humiliated by their parents, as children" (p. 99). In selected subjects, shame may have been shaped, in part, by parents' occasional sadistic pleasure in expressing disapproval by laughing at their children.

These actual experiences are assimilated into certain of the subject's superego compromise formations, where they contribute to their experience of that particular variety of guilt referred to as shame. It is worth noting that this contemporary understanding of shame is different from Freud's conception. Freud's ideas about shame were influenced by his ideas about important differences between men and women. Freud (1933) noted "we attribute a larger amount of narcissism to femininity" (p. 132), and continued, "the effect of penis-envy has a share . . . Shame, which is considered to be a feminine characteristic par excellence . . . has as its purpose . . . concealment of genital deficiency" (*ibid.*). The conception of shame presented in this paper conceives of men and women as more similar than different. Fantasies of deficiency are often associated with depressive affect and may, in selected subjects, be important aspects of the complex of compromise formations that constitute the superego. In certain women, penis envy may be associated with the experience of both shame and castration depressive affect. In working with such patients, the reconstruction of parental attitudes towards their children's gender and genitals may be important in understanding the development of their experience of envy, shame, and depressive affect.

The organizing impact of the oedipal phase on the calamities is stressed:

> Rivalrous incestuous and parenticidal drive derivatives have, as a part of their content, thoughts of object loss ("death wishes") and of loss of love ("fantasies of punishment and of retribution") as well as thoughts of castration. Psychoanalytic evidence shows that in every individual all three calamities participate in the anxiety and the depressive affect that initiate conflict in the oedipal period. [Brenner, 1982, p. 107]

Finally, Brenner's conception of the calamities has particular implications for the understanding of fantasies of castration. To the traditional conception of castration anxiety he has added the formulation of "castration depressive affect". Castration depressive affect is associated with the mortification a small boy experiences when he compares the size of his penis to that of his father's. It is also the affect a small girl experiences when she perceives she does not have a penis. In this regard, Brenner describes both the important relationship between depressive affect and identification functioning to reduce that unpleasure and important associated conflicts. He states, "depressive affect is often defended against . . . by identification with the aggressor, as evidenced by rage and by a wish for retributive (talion) revenge". He adds these "vengeful wishes themselves generate anxiety which must be warded off" (p. 103).

The Narcissistic Pursuit of Perfection

In *The Narcissistic Pursuit of Perfection* (Rothstein, 1980) my efforts at clarification focused on assimilating Freud's early conceptions of narcissism with *The Ego and the Id*. I stated that it is characteristic of Freud's seminal papers that central terms and concepts have a variety of meanings. Freud (1914a) defined narcissism as a quality of "perfection" (p. 94). In addition, he employed narcissism as a component of libido theory and used it metaphorically to describe aspects of human development from the perspective of libido development. In his prestructural metapsychological papers, Freud organized data within the libidinal concept of narcissism that would, subsequent to the introduction of the structural hypothesis, be discussed in terms of oral incorporative, defensive, and identificatory responses of the ego. Thus, Freud used the term narcissism to designate fantasies related to a felt quality of perfection and as a prestructural concept to describe the development of psychic structure in response to ubiquitous disappointments of childhood and the as yet undefined calamities of childhood. Both the ubiquitous frustrations and the calamities of childhood may be experienced as narcissistic injuries. Confusion has resulted from these two very different developments of the meaning of the term and concept narcissism.

I (1980) suggested that narcissism is different from the ego, the self, and the self-representation. These terms refer to hypothetical aspects of psychic structure, each with a characteristic development. I proposed that the definition of the term *narcissism* be limited to a *felt quality of perfection*. This conscious or unconscious affectively laden fantasy may be *invested* in a panoply of self and/or object representations in a *spectrum of integrations*.

Freud's prestructural conceptions of narcissism were pro-
pounded within the context of theory focused on libido and the
self-preservative instinct, prior to the introduction of the structural
hypothesis and the signal theory of anxiety. From this conceptual
perspective, narcissism was defined as the cathexis of the self with
narcissistic or ego libido, as contrasted with object libido. It was
considered as "a stage in the development of the libido which it
passes through on the way from auto-eroticism to object love"
(Freud, 1911, p. 60). I noted that in *The Ego and the Id* (1923), Freud
alluded to the metamorphosis of the libidinal concept, secondary
narcissism, into the structural concept, identification. He described
the development of the ego in the broadest sense, the development
of "character" (p. 28), as a response of the ego to the experience of
frustration. These limits are experienced by the subject as a narcissistic injury and as an object loss. The unpleasure associated with
these experiences motivates defensive internalizations that become
the fabric of the ego. Freud noted,

> We succeeded in explaining the painful disorder of melancholia by
> supposing that . . . an object which was lost has been set up again
> inside the ego, that is, that an object-cathexis has been replaced by
> an identification. [p. 28]

In 1923, Freud deleted the qualification of that identification as
"narcissistic". In 1915b, the exposition of the identification in melancholia as a "narcissistic identification" had been a central premise
and distinction of his explanation of the pathogenesis of that condition. In *The Ego and the Id*, he commented on this earlier hypothesis.

> At that time, however, we did not appreciate the full significance of
> this process and did not know how common and how typical it is.
> Since then we have come to understand that this kind of substitu-
> tion has a great share in determining the form taken by the ego and
> that it makes an essential contribution towards building up what is
> called "character" . . .

> At the very beginning . . . object cathexes and identification are no
> doubt indistinguishable . . . It may be that this identification is the
> sole condition under which the id can give up its objects . . . it [is]
> possible to suppose that the character of the ego is a precipitate of
> abandoned object-cathexes and that it contains the history of those
> object-choices. [pp. 28–29]

Freud's (1911, 1914a) libidinal delineation of the ubiquitous nature of secondary narcissism was a metaphorical precursor of his later object-representational formulation of the genesis of the "character of the ego" (1923, p. 28). Freud (1911) had defined primary narcissism as "a stage in the development of the libido which it passes through on the way from auto-erotism to object-love" (p. 60). In 1914b, he stated,

> The libido that has been withdrawn from the external world has been directed to the ego [self] and thus gives rise to an attitude which may be called narcissism . . . This leads us to look upon the narcissism which arises through the drawing in of object-cathexes as a secondary one, superimposed upon a primary narcissism that is obscured by a number of different influences. [p. 75]

The withdrawal of libido from an object representation to the "self", associated with a transformation of object libido to ego or narcissistic libido, is another metaphorical way of describing the process of identification with the disappointing or lost object. Prior to 1923, during the gestation of the structural hypotheses, with its corollary revision of the theory of anxiety, the term narcissism was employed to refer to processes of internalization that contribute to ego, ego-ideal, and superego development. It seems clarifying to employ Freud's 1923 representational description of identificatory processes and to dispense with the libidinal concept of secondary narcissism as a tool for organizing these developmental events.

In response to Adler, Freud (1914a) focused, for a brief moment, on "the disturbances to which a child's original narcissism is exposed" (p. 92). In a brief three and a half pages, Freud explored possible conflicts concerning vicissitudes of the loss of fantasies of perfection in early childhood contributing to the development of the ego ideal and the superego (pp. 93–94) as well as exploring parents' investments of fantasies of perfection in their children (p. 91). Freud noted that parents

> are under a compulsion to ascribe every perfection to the child . . . to conceal and forget all his shortcomings (incidentally, the denial of sexuality in children is connected with this) . . . illness, death, renunciation of enjoyment, restrictions on his own will, shall not touch him . . . At the most touchy point in the narcissistic system,

the immortality of the ego, which is so hard pressed by reality, security is achieved by taking refuge in the child. [p. 91]

Freud emphasized the ubiquitous life-long effort to undo the sense of loss of the original pleasurable fantasy of perfection and the use of that fantasy to defend against sexual conflicts and conflicts related to perceptions of one's finiteness. In 1926, he emphasized the inevitable association of these conflicts when he noted that, "the fear of death . . . is a fear of the superego projected on to the powers of destiny" (p. 140). I would add, in the context of Brenner's conceptualization, that the awareness of the decline of one's powers and of the disintegration of one's body is inevitably associatively linked to the castration depressive affect of formative Oedipal conflicts.

In regard to young children, Freud (1914a) suggested that the child's "original narcissism" (p. 94), their original fantasies of perfection, are preserved in the formation of the ego ideal. Freud stated,

> man has here again shown himself incapable of giving up a satisfaction he had once enjoyed. He is not willing to forgo narcissistic perfection of his childhood . . . he seeks to recover it in the new form of the ego ideal. [*ibid.*]

Freud (1933) subsequently subsumed this striving within his evolving structural conception of the superego, noting that the superego "is also the vehicle of the ego ideal by which the ego measures itself, which it emulates, and whose demand for ever greater perfection it strives to fulfil" (pp. 64–65). Freud continued, "The super-ego is the representative for us of every moral restriction, the advocate of a striving towards perfection—it is . . . the higher side of human life" (pp. 66–67).

It is from this perspective that I suggested a more limited definition of narcissism as a fantasy of perfection. I noted that the quality of perfection may be consciously perceived or may be an unconsciously active, affectively valent fantasy. In addition, I noted that the phrase "fantasy of perfection" is employed as a generalization. Fantasies of perfection are expressed in ideas of omniscience or omnipotence. A subject or object is thought of as most knowing, most powerful, most beautiful, most successful, etc. What is common to all is a superlative designation, such as "most" and the absolute quality of this designation. Fantasies of perfection are also associated with the number "one" and often with the wish to be "one and only". Fantasies of perfection are a ubiquitous aspect of human experience that facilitate distortion of one's sense of reality, particularly as this relates to one's sense of vulnerability and finiteness. These fantasies differ from person to person in their elaboration and integration by the ego.

Like Freud, I speculated on the origins of fantasies of perfection in the pre-individuated era and emphasized its relationship to psychic conflict at all stages of life. In *Civilization and Its Discontents*, Freud (1930) described the defensive use of fantasies of perfection and their implicit relationship to very early experiences of helplessness, as well as to later childhood fantasies of genital inferiority.

> With every tool man is perfecting his own organs . . . or is removing the limits to their functioning . . . These things . . . man has brought about on this earth, on which he first appeared as a feeble animal organism . . . as a helpless suckling. [pp. 90–91]

In the same paragraph Freud continued,

> Long ago he formed an ideal conception of omnipotence and omniscience which he embodied in the gods . . . Today [through "his science and technology" (p. 91)] he has come very close to the attainment of his ideal. [p. 91]

Finally, from a perspective in striking accord with Brenner's (1982) emphasis on the ubiquity of psychic conflict in normality and pathology, I (1980) stressed that the definition of narcissism as a fantasy of perfection is a unitary one. Its existence in mental life provides a ubiquitous distorting influence. "Its loss is a ubiquitous developmental insult from which few, if any, human beings recover" (*ibid.*, p. 72). Again, in accord with Brenner's distinction between normal and pathologic compromise formations as defined by the degree of unpleasure characterized by each, I (1980) noted in regard to fantasies of perfection that

> the pursuit of narcissistic perfection in one form or another is a defensive distortion that is a ubiquitous characteristic of the mind.

It is a goal of analysis to identify the nature of the analysand's narcissistic investments and to work on those aspects of the investments that contribute to suffering and maladaption. It is questionable whether the total relinquishment of narcissistic perfection is possible or desirable. [*ibid.*, pp. 22–23]

Fantasies of perfection

The focus of this section of the chapter is on some relationships between fantasies of perfection and the calamities of childhood. Several related propositions are explored, as listed below.

1. A fantasy of perfection is best thought of as a compromise formation composed of drive derivatives, unpleasurable affects, defence and superego elements interacting. Because analysis of a fantasy of perfection typically reveals a series of related fantasies, in every case one finds many different drive derivatives, many fears and miseries, many defences in the underlying conflict(s).
2. Fantasies of perfection have a development that is influenced, in part, by the development of the calamities of childhood.
3. Fantasies of perfection function as defences to diminish unpleasure associated with conflict. From this perspective, a fantasy of perfection is a component of compromise formations.
4. The threat of the loss of the fantasy of perfection evokes anxiety, while the sense the loss has occurred is associated with the experience of depressive affect.
5. Fantasies of perfection are important aspects of the compromise formations that constitute subjects' consciences. They are also important components of masochistic and narcissistic compromise formations characteristic of aspects of character. These compromise formations are intimately related to defensive identificatory relationships between the self (as-agent) and subjects' consciences.

It is a premise of this chapter that fantasies of perfection develop in synchrony with the fantasies that are the ideational contents of the calamities of childhood and are employed by the mind to diminish the unpleasure characteristic of these calamities. Freud's (1920) description of his grandson's pleasurable play in the service of diminishing the unpleasure associated with his mother's departure suggests just such a defensive relationship. His grandson engaged in play that was associated with the fantasy of undoing the loss of the object. I am suggesting the conjecture that, in the "joyful 'da'" (p. 15) associated with the play, a fantasy of perfection was restored to his grandson's self-representation. Similarly, when a subject experiences unpleasure associated with the sense that love will be or is lost, fantasies of undoing the calamity may be associated with a sense that the subject is perfect and, therefore, lovable.

Analogously, when castration is threatened, or seems to have occurred, subjects may attempt to undo the sense of calamity by imagining they have a penis (Rado, 1933) or by imagining they can seduce (Loewenstein, 1957) or defeat the castrator. Similar fantasies characterize aspects of the child's masochistic and narcissistic (Rothstein, 1984) responses to the calamity of imminent punishment.

As with the calamities of childhood, once the Oedipal epoch occurs, all the calamities and associated fantasies of perfection are integrally interwoven and, thus, inseparable. As a generalization, an adult's fantasies of perfection bear a relationship to all the calamities of childhood. However, as with drive derivatives and affects, each individual's fantasies of perfection have "a uniquely personal history . . . form . . . and content" (Brenner, 1982, p. 26).

Brenner (1982) has noted the relationship between depressive affect and identification with the aggressor. In considering the development of Freud's prestructural conceptions of defensive narcissistic identification and his (1923) subsequent conception of identification, one is struck by the advantage of elaborating them using Brenner's concept of depressive affect. Freud's (1917b) formulation of melancholia can now be elaborated: the sense that a calamity has occurred is associated with the experience of depressive affect, which triggers conflict and the creation of the fantasy of the lost object within the self. Similarly, Freud's (1923) formulation of the genesis of the "character of the ego" can now be elaborated: "When a person has to give up a sexual object" (p. 29), the person experiences depressive affect, which triggers conflict and the

ensu[ing] alteration of the self which can only be described as a
setting up of the object inside the self . . . It may be that this identification is the sole condition under which the id can give up its
objects. [*ibid.*]

In a similar vein, the concept of depressive affect facilitates an
elaborated appreciation of Freud's (1926) description of typical
danger situations as well as of the experience of the loss of the fantasy of perfection. Many of the subjects that Freud dealt with under
the rubric of narcissism had to do with fantasies that a calamity had
occurred. The lack of a satisfactory dynamic conceptualization with
regard to unpleasurable depressive states may have interfered with
Freud's ability to assimilate his theoretical constructions of narcissism within his subsequent structural model.

Fantasies of perfection are important aspects of the compromise
formations that constitute what Freud termed "the superego". The
origins of the subject's ideals have been placed in the second year
of life. However, once the child enters the Oedipal phase of life,
living up to his ideals and winning his parents' approval are
inevitably linked to conflicts concerning the sexual and murderous
wishes that characterize that epoch. I am suggesting that for a child,
the sense of being able to win parental approval and love through
performance, or the sense of having manipulated, controlled,
seduced, or defeated the punisher, often fantasized as sadistic and
omnipotent, is associated with the conscious and/or unconscious
fantasy that the subject is omnipotent.

In elaboration of Eidelberg (1959) and Bergler (1961), I (1983,
1984, 1988) have described the unconscious narcissistic gratifications that are aspects of masochistic fantasies employed in the
service of defence. When a subject imposes pain on himself, he is
gratified by the unconscious fantasy that, in identification with the
aggressor, he is imposing the pain on another. The subject feels that
he is triumphing over the aggressive punishing parental imago
conceived of as sadistic and omnipotent. I am emphasizing that in
this fantasized triumph, a fantasy of perfection is temporarily
restored to the self-as-agent.

Similarly, a subject may fantasize more overt and manifest
defeat of a punishing parental imago. Such triumph is, similarly,
associated with the fantasy that perfection is restored to the self-as-

agent. Brenner (1982) alluded to this relationship when he stated, "Depending on the intensity of the pleasure and the nature of the associated ideas, one may speak of a variety of triumph as omnipotence" (p. 45).

Clinical material and discussion

Dr D, a plastic surgeon, was obsessed with the conscious fantasy of perfecting his circumcised penis by performing an autocircumcision. He experienced this obsession and its enactment with a mixture of excitement and apprehension not unlike that associated with behaviour designated counterphobic. Analysis revealed defensive relationships between this conscious fantasy of creating a perfect penis and a number of the calamities of childhood: object loss depressive affect, loss of love anxiety, depressive affect and castration anxiety, and castration depressive affect. In addition, analysis revealed the associated unconscious wish to be a woman, which was defensively related to the calamities of his childhood.

Dr D's mother had deeply wished he were born a girl. As a toddler, he was dressed in girl's clothing, and his mother repeatedly hurt him as she painfully cleaned his uncircumcised penis. She threatened Dr D often with circumcision if he failed to keep his penis clean. Dr D related numerous dreams where castration was clearly represented. On a lonely weekend that was the first anniversary of his mother's death, he performed a circumcision on his already circumcised penis. This act was associated with the conscious fantasy that he was endeavouring to make his penis perfect so he could be more attractive to men in the baths. This dramatic enactment was repeated in the transference in response to my leaving him during the third year of his analysis. The transferential significance and displacement were interpreted. In his loneliness, he was trying to make himself more acceptable not only to men, but to me as his mother, more specifically by symbolically castrating himself and thereby making himself into a woman. The relationship between this dramatic enactment and his wish to be a woman was clear in a manifest dream reported in response to my cancelling a Friday hour. On Monday he reported,

> Last night I dreamt I was in my bedroom, but it was furnished like this office. I was in bed masturbating. My mother was down the hall in her bedroom. I was afraid she'd catch me. I got the urge to perfect my circumcision by taking every last bit of skin off, but I recognized if I did that there would be no more skin on the shaft and the head of the penis would be pinned down like a clitoris. A man came through the window with a knife and I woke up in terror. Then I had an obsession to see your penis.

Dr D's father worked long hours. He would come home tired and lie in bed with Dr D for hours. Lying together, Dr D and his father would comb each other's hair. He remembers these moments warmly.

Dr D's dramatic enactments were understood to be motivated by defensive efforts to diminish object loss depressive affect and guilt associated with the anniversary of his mother's death and with the temporary loss of his analyst. The conscious fantasy of the perfect penis and the associated unconscious wish to be a woman were organized, in addition and in part, in defensive relationship to other calamities of his childhood. Loss of love anxiety and depressive affect, as well as castration anxiety, were responses to drive derivatives whose development was influenced by his experience of his mother's hostility towards his penis as well as by his perception of his mother's explicit, and father's implicit, wish that he be a girl. The defensive employment of "identification with the aggressor (castrator)" (A. Freud, 1936) and "seduction of the aggressor" (Loewenstein, 1957) can be seen to be additional defensive aspects of the compromise formations that comprise the organization of the fantasies that motivated the enactment. Related self-punitive contributions to these fantasies seem clear.

Mr X, a lawyer, has been obsessed with bitterness and rage at his parents as well as with wishes for revenge.

Data are presented from a five-month period in the sixth year of his second analysis that demonstrate some relationships between fantasies of perfection and the calamities of his childhood. In particular, the data demonstrate the subject's effort to reduce his experience of depressive affect by pursuing fantasies of perfection.

Mr X began a session, two weeks before my summer vacation, by stating,

"For some reason I'm on this crusade to be perfect and I can't let it go. If the dinner I'm cooking doesn't turn out well I have a minor temper tantrum. When I ask myself what I enjoy, well, I enjoy skiing; but what I really enjoy is being admired from the chair lift. I think it's that I want everything. My firm is so competitive. I respond with perfectionism and it robs me of any pleasure in it. I'm so angry I can't let it go."

I interpreted: "You're angry you're not declared the winner by birthright." Mr X responded, "Yeah, something like that. I think of my father not inviting me into his firm." I commented: "You believe that if you were perfect you could make your father want you to be a colleague."

Mr X responded, "Yeah, I still have that fantasy. I feel like I'd have paid any price and would now be in my firm. I suppose I do the same thing in analysis. I spent a fortune in time and money with Dr M and now I'm doing the same thing here in pursuit of the same fantasy. Most people would say, 'Well you went through one really long analysis, try something else'. All I do is come around to the same damn fantasy. I find yet another way to delude myself that if I only do the right thing I'll get my father's attention. It seems like the alternative is to be as depressed as hell. To give up this omnipotent fantasy. To give up the fantasy that if only I played my cards right I'd get his love. It feels like death. I cannot let myself feel what it feels like. It's as if thinking of the pain doesn't let one try. Thinking of being number one and wanting it and not getting it is too painful so I say I don't really want it."

Three months later, Mr X was struggling mightily to diminish the sadness he was feeling in response to his awareness that he was making progress in his analysis. He began a session by pondering the paradox of the sadness he felt in response to his professional success. I interpreted: "You experience your success as a reminder of all the things you can't be and can't have." Mr X associated, "I say a resounding 'No!' to the idea of loss and disappointment. It's like some electric shock I can't consider inflicting on myself and then I think you think it bothers me and I say nothing bothers me 'cause I'm the greatest." Mr X paused, and continued, "One of the things about accepting I can't change the past and about growing up would be I'll stop coming here and won't be with you any more." Mr X associated to other losses, and then said, "The idea that there are choices and that means leaving things behind and missing them every day I find unacceptable. It's like I won't be sad every day. I refuse! Then I get blocked." After a few moments of silence, he said, "I immediately put the whole thing in terms of some kind of humiliation." I interpreted, "You create a humiliator who you imagine you can beat. You imagine if you defeat the humiliator you won't have to deal with disappointment or loss." Mr X responded, "I can really feel that and sense wanting to turn that into revenge and finally getting even . . . The alternative is to say there's just loss, just disappointment. It's partly because I feel there is no comfort for that. Then I think there is comfort in going forward . . . It's a measure of how much I still want from my parents that makes the idea of progress seem so bitter."

In the ensuing weeks, I was able to interpret Mr X's narcissistically invested fantasies that if he did the correct thing he would be able to undo the frustrations of his life in general and those of his Oedipal experience in particular. The analysis of his experience of frustration in the transference was a particularly helpful vehicle in this interpretive process.

Mr X began a session six weeks after the one reported by saying, "The idea that I had this operational fantasy that if I just worked hard enough I'd win my mother and have her all to myself seems crazy but right—so right! Today I feel myself in a real funk. It's as if I figured all the angles and still couldn't get my mother's love. Rather than just conclude that and say there are other things in life, I feel there must be something I'm doing wrong and if I can only figure it out, I'll get my mother and be OK."

Mr X's associations shifted to the fact that the Christmas and New Year's holidays prevented him from having five analytic sessions during those weeks. He stated, "There being two three day weekends in a row. I take it so personally. It's a three-day weekend for the entire United States and I take it as a personal failure and humiliation to not be able to get an appointment on Monday and a humiliation that I can't get a senior partner to treat me as a special son and a humiliation that I can't get my mother's love. I have to brood over it rather than just say that's the way the cards fell. Why do I feel I'll die when I don't feel I have the power, the control?"

Mr X was silent for a while, then said, "Being a lawyer is satisfying in and of itself, but right now I feel so bitter. I can't win her love and that's just a recognition that I'm not omnipotent. So I'd like to say just go on and pursue your own interests but all day I feel angry choking humiliation. So it was just a fantasy and that's what it was."

Mr X paused, and I interpreted: "You're experiencing a double disappointment. You sense the loss of the possibility of having your mother all to yourself and the loss of your belief that you had the power to make it happen." Mr X responded, "The humiliation feels like shitting in my pants. I know my mother was enraged to clean my shit. Nothing I could do as a kid could make them love me. I stand back and look at it. It feels so bad so I revert to saying you can't hurt me."

In conclusion, I wish to reiterate the clinical value of analysing fantasies of perfection as compromise formations. In this chapter, I have emphasized the defensive function of fantasies of perfection and the relationship between the development of these fantasies and the calamities of childhood. Because of the latter relationship, analysis of fantasies of perfection inevitably reveals associative links to conflicts concerning childhood sexual and aggressive desires. It is not uncommon, in the analysis of fantasies of perfection, to uncover associated bisexual fantasies. These, too, are analysed as compromise formations and also function, in part, defensively. In men, these fantasies may be expressed as the wish to be a woman, while in women they may be expressed as the wish to be a man. In both men and women fantasies of perfection and bisexual fantasies are not infrequently associated with fantasies of repair of a fantasized sense of defect and/or castration.

CHAPTER THREE

Sadomasochism

This chapter explores the advantages of considering the varieties of expressions of sadomasochism from the theoretical perspective that suggests these phenomena are best understood as compromise formations. From this perspective all data referred to as sadomasochistic are thought to derive from conscious and/or unconscious fantasies. They include the explicit enactments of the perversions, the subtle, less obvious expressions of character, or the painful, self-torturing, obsessive fantasies characteristic of some neurotic preoccupations. These fantasies, like all fantasies in adults, are conceived of as compromise formations constructed of the contributions of drive derivatives, affects, defences, and self-punitive trends. This theoretical perspective emphasizes the dynamic point of view while de-emphasizing certain descriptive designations and some of their diagnostic implications. Thus, the organizing descriptive designations—perversion, character and neurosis—lose some of their value and these phenomena are appreciated as being on a spectrum and as more similar than different.

I shall explore neurotic aspects of an analysand's experience, emphasizing the expression of sadomasochism in neurotic symptomatology and inhibition.

Theoretical considerations

In addition to defining masochism descriptively, as Freud (1905a) did, as pleasure in physical pain or in the pain associated with experiences of humiliation or subjugation, when one defines it theoretically as a compromise formation, a number of advantages ensue. Freud (1894) early described a neurotic symptom as a compromise among a wish, a defence, and a desire for self-punishment. His (1923, 1926) later theoretical elaborations emphasized the contributions of the wish for punishment and the signal function of anxiety to the structure of neurotic symptomatology. Numerous analysts have applied this perspective and contributed to its evolution.

Brenner's (1982) contribution is important in several ways. First, it emphasized the ubiquity of conflict in normality and pathology. He stressed that conflict and "compromise formation [are] a general tendency of the mind, not an exceptional one" (p. 113). Thus, all data in adults are derived from fantasies. In this sense, normality and pathology are similar in their shared constituents. Their differences are related to certain descriptive, experiential, and adaptive characteristics:

> a compromise formation is pathological when it is characterized by any combination of the following features: too much restriction of gratification of drive derivatives, too much inhibition of functional capacity, too much unpleasure—i.e., too much conscious anxiety, depressive affect, or both—too great a tendency to injure or to destroy oneself, or too great conflict with one's environment. [*ibid.*, p. 150]

Second, Brenner underlined the importance of numerous factors in the creation of a neurotic symptom in an adult, and, thereby, facilitates a neutral attitude towards the data, lessening the tendency towards oversimplified unifactoral explanations:

> ... one must keep in mind the complexities involved if one is to follow the full range of the analytic material of any patient. One must be prepared to see evidence of misery alternating with terror, of terror breeding misery, of loss of love implying castration, of castration depressive affect leading to object loss, and of all the

other combinations of the ideational content of the calamities of childhood that characterize psychic life in the oedipal phase of development. It is only by being prepared for these complex inter-relations that one can hope to catch the evidence for each of them as it appears in a given patient's analytical material. [*ibid.*, p. 108]

Third, and relatedly, Brenner distinguished between a theoretical conception of development in very young children and the understanding of meanings of adult analytic data. He emphasized the importance of influences from all phases of development, stressing, as Freud did, the organizing influence of the Oedipal phase on earliest experiences. With regard to the calamities of childhood, Brenner stated,

Rivalrous incestuous and parenticidal drive derivatives have, as a part of their content, thoughts of object loss (= death wishes) and of loss of love (= fantasies of punishment and of retribution) as well as thoughts of castration. Psychoanalytic evidence shows that in every individual all three calamities participate in the anxiety and depressive affect that initiate conflict in the oedipal period. [*ibid.*, p. 107].

This theoretical perspective is particularly important in contrasting the point of view expressed in this chapter to the points of view of other contributors to the subject of sadomasochism. For example, Bergler (1961) offered a unifactorial pre-Oedipal reconstruction to explain the genesis and dynamics of masochism in adults. He stated,

It is my contention that the first and foremost conflict of the newborn, infant, baby, consists in the fact that he must come to terms with his inborn megalomania. That conflict invariably and without exception results in a masochistic solution, the "pleasure-in-displeasure" pattern. This constitutes the "basic neurosis". [p. 63]

From Brenner's perspective, there is no exclusively pre-Oedipal pathology. In adults, pathology of all types bears the influences of all stages of development: pre-Oedipal, Oedipal, and post Oedipal. From this point of view it is inexact, oversimplified, and misleading to conceive of certain perversions as pre-Oedipal and of the neuroses as Oedipal in origin.

Finally, Brenner's elaboration of depressive affect as a component of compromise formations is an original conceptualization that is helpful in considering the complex of pathological compromise formations that underlie neurotic symptoms, character traits, and perverse enactments. This conceptualization is particularly relevant to the subject of this chapter because of the important relation between masochism and depression (Rothstein, 1983, pp. 130–131). Most previous contributions (Bergler, 1961; Berliner, 1940; Olinick, 1964) have stressed pre-Oedipal factors in the genesis of this relation. More specifically, they emphasize the calamity of object loss and the related conception of narcissistic injury as akin to the loss of a fantasied relationship to a narcissistic (and sadistic) object. Brenner's (1982) conceptualization integrates all the calamities of childhood and adds the clinically valuable concept "castration depressive affect" (p. 108).

When one considers masochistic symptomatology in adults from the theoretical perspective that conceives of the phenomena as compromise formations, two separate but related points are emphasized. One is that in every case one finds drive derivatives, unpleasurable affects, defence, and self-punitive elements interacting. The other is that in every case one finds complex combinations of many different drive derivatives, many fears and miseries, many defences, and many self-punitive manifestations in the underlying conflicts.

It is also important to note that masochistic fantasies are always associated with conscious and/or unconscious sadistic and narcissistic fantasies that are, like masochistic fantasies in adults, best thought of as compromise formations. The masochistic pleasure in pain, humiliation, and subjugation is always associated with the sadistic pleasure in hurting, humiliating, subjugating, and/or extracting revenge, as well as with narcissistic fantasies of orchestrating the scenario and of being the omnipotent humiliator, subjugator, and/or revenger.

Finally, brief comments on some other aspects of the literature on masochism are indicated. In my previous contributions to this subject, the multiplicity of factors that comprise phenomena described as masochistic were stressed. I noted (1983) that "Although most authors note its overdetermined nature, they stressed one or another aspect of masochistic phenomena in their explications" (p. 107). I emphasized the narcissistic dynamic in masochism, stressing defence and the value of a representational perspective in theoretical conceptualizations. With regard to ideas concerning the dynamic relation of narcissism to masochism, our debt to Bergler (1961), Eidelberg (1959), and Cooper (1977, unpublished) is noteworthy. Although it is beyond the scope of this paper to review the literature in a comprehensive manner, it is important to note a series of contributions (Berliner, 1940, 1942, 1947, 1958; Socarides, 1958; Valenstein, 1973) that stress the influence of the hateful sadistic object world in the genesis of masochism. Berliner's contributions are seminal in this regard. He stresses (1958) that masochism is "a disturbance of object relations, a pathologic way of loving a person who gives hate and ill-treatment" (p. 40). In discussing the fear of humiliation in the tradition of Berliner, I stated (1984) "The influence of the pleasure of the parental object in sadistically humiliating is emphasized in the overdetermined genesis of this fear" (p. 115).

This chapter stresses the theoretical perspective that fantasies in adults can best be understood as compromise formations. From this perspective, the influence of the object world in the genesis of masochistic, narcissistic, and sadistic fantasies in adults is understood as its contribution in shaping an individual's character. *The real objects of a person's world influence the content of the fantasies that constitute that person's drive derivatives, affects, defences, and self-punitive tendencies.*

Analytic data is presented from a case in which the pathological compromise formations that underlie the patient's masochism contribute to its expression in neurotic symptoms, character traits, and perverse enactments. The data presented stress its expression in neurotic symptomatology.

Case presentation

Mr X is a thirty-four-year-old, married, successful lawyer. Psychic pain was prominent in his symptomatology. He began the first session of the week in the fifth year of his second analysis by reporting humiliating aspects of a weekend event, in an agitated manner. On this day, his discomfort was more acute than was usual for him. The psychic pain in his agitation was particularly impressive to me. I understood his agitation on this occasion to reflect an intense experience of anxiety and depressive affect related to his fantasies of both fearing humiliation and feeling humiliated.

> Mr X began his session by reporting, "I was called by my uncle's wife at 10 p.m. on Saturday night and told he had been arrested and was being held by the police. I told her I would go to the precinct and get him released. On the way there I became obsessed with the idea that everyone at the precinct would think my uncle was my homosexual lover. I know that has to do with you. When I arrived at the precinct it became clear to everyone that I was a person of influence with the power to make them uncomfortable. They were very courteous, and I was able to get my uncle released on bail without any difficulty. While I was there I had to let them all know I was married. I was terrified they'd think I was gay."

In response to his manifest masochistic fantasy of anticipating feeling humiliatingly embarrassed, my ensuing interpretation emphasized a defensive aspect of the compromise formation. I commented, "You felt quite potent in the way you were able to help your uncle." Mr X said "Yes," and was silent for a while. I interpreted, "Your painful fantasy helped you diminish the frightening sense you were quite a man."

Despite the fact that Mr X is a highly respected professional and an excellent athlete, he has been characteristically unable to experience and report satisfaction and pride in his accomplishments at work or in sports. However, in response to the interpretation, he spent the next twenty minutes describing his joy in his skills at work and at play. With glee, he said, "I'm good at a lot of things." After a moment I responded, "You're enjoying feeling potent at work." He agreed. His associations shifted to a friend whose competitive wishes prevented him from acknowledging Mr X's skills. Mr X stated, "The son of a bitch could acknowledge what a good lawyer I am. I literally wanted to blow him away." His associations shifted to his lifelong experience of his father as indifferent and denigrating. Mr X stated, "There is a part of me that just wanted to brag . . . I really want this guy to say 'you're the greatest'. I thought how when I was an adolescent my father once said my cousin was amazing, and I was so jealous. He never said that about me."

Mr X began the next session by asking me if I could change the time of a session the following week. He went on to say that he was thinking about how much easier it was to accept yesterday's interpretation than it had been to accept other interpretations concerning his wishes towards his father. Mr X paused. I understood him to be referring to the painful work we had done on his wish to be my homosexual lover as well as his wish to be a woman and have our baby. These wishes had been interpreted in both their negative and positive Oedipal contexts. With regard to the latter, his wish to be a woman was associated with an adolescent masturbatory fantasy that his mother was bisexual and they were lesbian lovers.

He then reported that his father was having professional difficulties. His request for a change of appointment was required because a number of family members were gathering to consider what might be done to improve his father's situation. He reported details of his father's failings as a lawyer and, jokingly, said, "I am having a fantasy of taking over Dad's failing firm and making it a success." I commented, "You sound as if you think you are ready." He said, "Yeah" joyfully, and paused. His mood became more serious, and he associated to the story of a boy who killed himself after his father called him an upstart for being critical of him. I interpreted, "You would like to be more potent than your father and replace him." Mr X said, "Yeah. I understand that. Trying to think about it makes me very anxious. What I really want is to punish him for my disappointments as a child, to kill him."

Discussion

From the organizing theoretical perspective that conceives of Mr X's masochism as comprising a complex of fantasies that are each best understood as a compromise formation, the analytic data from the two sessions presented in this paper can be understood to reflect Mr X's conflicts concerning his sexual and aggressive wishes towards his parents.

The patient began his session by reporting his masochistic fear of being humiliated. He did this against a background of hard-won analytic insight concerning both his wish to be humiliated and his wish to be a homosexual and a woman. These fantasies had been understood and repeatedly interpreted as compromise formations, resulting in a reduction of the agitated depressive unpleasure that characterized his personality.

In the sessions reported here, the interpretations focused on the defensive aspect of one of these compromise formations: his fear–wish to be humiliated in the police station. The choice to emphasize the defensive function of the compromise formation was probably related to work on Mr X's sado-narcissistic competitive feelings toward his father. Their emergence and intensification at this time were related, in part, to exigencies in his father's life. It is important to emphasize that the theoretical perspective employed in this paper stresses that this masochistic fantasy had significance other than being merely defensive. Sexual and aggressive wishes as well as related wishes for punishment contribute to the organization of masochistic fantasies. These aspects of Mr X's masochistic fantasies had been interpreted in other sessions. An example of such work occurred in the second year of the analysis. Mr X reported that during my summer vacation he had been plagued by the fantasy that he had AIDS. Analysis revealed both the wish for the experience of sexual love with the analyst as well as the wish to hurt and punish the analyst and himself. The latter self-punitive wish was understood to reflect, in part, his guilt related to the drive derivatives gratified in his painful fantasy of infection with the human immunodeficiency virus.

In a sense, it is a tactical decision that determines which aspect of a compromise formation an analyst chooses to interpret in a given session or series of sessions. The work in the two sessions presented here facilitated a diminution of the symptomatic unpleasure associated with his fear of being humiliated and facilitated his more conscious experience of his positive Oedipal competitive strivings. Specifically, Mr X became more aware of a series of libidinal and aggressive wishes (his sado-exhibitionistic fantasy of bragging, his sado-narcissistic desire for vengeance, and his wish to compete with and to kill his father). Mr X became more aware of how anxious these wishes made him. His associations to the story of the boy who killed himself after criticizing his father emphasize the self-punitive tendencies that are an important element of his conflict concerning his wishes to humiliate, hurt, and kill his father. Insight concerning these wishes diminished the unpleasure, primarily anxiety and guilt, associated with them as well as the related need to create a humiliating masochistic fantasy in the service, in part, of diminishing that unpleasure. These data also reflect the organizing influence of his father's indifference and sadism and his mother's exhibitionism in contributing a shaping element to Mr X's sado-narcissistic and sadomasochistic fantasies.

Although positive Oedipal libidinal drive derivatives were not present in Mr X's associations, previous analysis had delineated their contribution to the complex of compromise formations considered in these hours.

An additional comment is in order on the relationship of depression and narcissism to sadomasochism. Bernstein (1957), Berliner (1958), Bergler (1961), and particularly Olinick (1964) have alerted us to the important relation of masochism to depression. Olinick made explicit what Bergler had implied: that masochistic fantasies can be employed defensively to help diminish depressive affect. I have emphasized (1983) the defensive function of masochistic fantasies in diminishing the depressive affect associated with the fantasy that the sadistic object has been lost. In addition, I have stressed that depressive affect is experienced in response to the loss of the narcissistically gratifying fantasy of being able to control the sadistic object. As noted previously, Brenner's elaboration of the concept compromise formation adds breadth to these contributions. Masochistic fantasies can be employed to diminish depressive affect associated with the sense that any of the calamities of childhood have occurred; that is, masochistic fantasies may be employed to diminish the depressive affect associated with the sense that the object has been lost, that its love has been lost, that castration has occurred, and that one is bad and punishment is required. These fantasies diminish the depressive affect because their content temporarily undoes the sense of calamity. For example, object loss depressive affect may be diminished by creating the sense of the presence of the [sadistic] object, while loss of love depressive affect may be diminished by the creation of the sense that the sadistic object loves the masochistic subject. Relatedly, masochistic fantasies may be employed to diminish the depressive affect associated with the sense that the subject has lost the illusion of his perfectibility.

Mr X and I have come to understand aspects of his character as serving to defend against an admixture of depressive affect tinged with the unpleasure of anxiety, which often contributes an agitated quality to his depressive affect. Mr X's depressive affect has been understood to comprise, in part, object love depressive affect, an aspect of which is the sense that his father did not love him. His humiliating fantasies of being a homosexual and a woman have been understood as triggered in part by the admixture of anxiety and depressive affect associated with his sense of losing—having lost—his father's love.

When one considers Mr X's humiliating fantasies of being a homosexual and/or a woman from the theoretical perspective that understands them as compromise formations, a number of the elements of Mr X's underlying conflicts are clarified. These fantasies express Mr X's sexual and aggressive wishes towards his parents. At the same time, they serve to diminish the unpleasure associated with both these wishes and related self-punitive trends.

In the sessions reported in this chapter, the humiliating fantasy of being a homosexual was understood to be related primarily to Mr X's competitive wish to kill and succeed his father. This wish evoked anxiety and guilt, which triggered a humiliating homosexual fantasy intended to diminish that unpleasure. My interpretation, "Your painful fantasy helped you diminish the frightening sense you were quite a man," emphasized the defensive component of the compromise formation. Mr X's associations confirmed the correctness of the interpretation and revealed other elements of the compromise formation, as well as related wishes for his father's love, his depressing sense of the loss of that love, and his sadistic wish for vengeance.

Narcissistic gratification is one aspect of the complex of compromise formations that underlie all sadomasochistic experiences. These narcissistic fantasies of perfection may remain unconscious and unanalysed in work with many symptomatic expressions of sadomasochism. Narcissistic aspects of masochism are more likely to be analysed when one is working with tenaciously held self-destructive aspects of a patient's personality. It is particularly helpful to focus on the narcissistic fantasies in masochistic enactments when one finds oneself pondering the question, "How could he do that to himself?" (Rothstein, 1983, 1984). In elaboration of Freud's (1917b) insight that "the ego can . . . treat itself as an object" (p. 252), I (1983, 1988) have suggested that a narcissistically invested "I", a self-as-agent, which feels itself to be invulnerable and immortal, is imposing the pain on the "me", conceptualized as a self-as-object. (Schafer [1968] delineated the distinctions between "self-as-agent" ["I"], self-as-object" ["me"], and "self-as-place" [no pronoun].) The patient says, "I shall hurt or kill myself." There is no language that allows expression of the wish to hurt or kill the "I". One cannot say,

"I kill I-self." In addition, further analysis often reveals the fantasied presence of objects in the associations to the idea of the "me", which helps one better to understand the fantasized imposition of pain by the "I" upon the objects who exist in fantasy within the "me".

This perspective was particularly useful in helping Mr X understand a profoundly frustrating and humiliating perverse acting out which occurred in his first analysis. In response to being left by his analyst, Mr X engaged in a brief homosexual affair. Among the multiple determinants of this enactment, Mr X became aware of the pleasurable fantasy of being able to control the presence of the object and of narcissistic gratifications associated with the expression of his rage towards both his analyst and his father. The invulnerable "I" in his personality had the illusion that he was imposing the humiliating experiences on them. In addition, he had the gratification of loving and of being loved by them in this way.

CHAPTER FOUR

Shame and guilt

T he purpose of this chapter is to stress the clinical advantages in the analyses of adults of considering the similarities between shame and guilt. The insight into their similarities is an extension of Brenner's (1982) elaboration of the "calamities of childhood" (p. 93) and his conception of the superego both as a component of a compromise formation and as composed of complexes of compromise formations.

Freud's conceptions of affects begin with a descriptive perspective that emphasizes their manifest differences. This starting point is in the tradition of Darwin's *Expression of the Emotions* (1872) and stresses the biological, adaptive, and inherited foundations of affects.

Freud emphasized guilt as one of the triggers of conflict. He considered shame and disgust to be related anti-instinctual elements of conflict. Since Adler's emphasis on feelings of inferiority, others have stressed the distinctions between shame and guilt, generally from a developmental perspective that emphasizes the relationship of shame to pre-Oedipal conflicts and conflictual issues around narcissism and self-esteem. More recent contributions have stressed conflicts between the ego and ego-ideal, considered to be triggered by shame, as contrasted with conflicts between the ego and superego, thought to be triggered by guilt. Freud's (1923, 1940) formulation of the superego as the product of identification with parents' moral authority, occurring as a consequence of the Oedipal stage of development, and his (1926) related concept of guilt as the final achievement of signal affect development, have been employed to support hypotheses that stress significant theoretical distinctions between shame and guilt.

Brenner's (1982) conception of the superego both as a component of a compromise formation and as composed of groups of compromise formations facilitates a consideration of shame and guilt as participants in the complex of compromise formations (that is, of fantasies) that constitute the superego.

The concept of the superego refers to the many fantasies concerning morality and ideals. These fantasies consist of ideas of what is correct or incorrect behaviour and what is ideal behaviour. From this vantage point, shame and guilt refer to fantasied types of parental disapproval. In this chapter, I emphasize that the clinically valuable distinctions between shame and guilt in adults are *descriptive* and are related to the fantasies associated with each affective experience. In a recent paper, Yorke and colleagues (1990) made a similar point. They stated, "Analysts have had a great deal to say about shame but . . . much of what they have said is descriptive rather than analytic" (p. 377). Both shame and guilt involve fantasies of what others thought, think, and/or will think of the subject. In guilt, however, the subject experiences a more conscious sense of personal responsibility. His or her experience remains more one of the subject-as-agent, the "I", feeling guilty for a wished for or imagined transgression. If the subject expressed this aspect of the experience of guilt, he or she might say, "I feel guilty, bad, and disapprove of what I wish to do, feel I have done, and/or have actually done."

In shame, an aspect of the content of a subject's conscious experience evokes the idea that parental disapproval is associated with being judged bad, inferior, or below standard in regard to some quality or capacity. The fantasy of shameful disapproval may be associated with ideas of being laughed at, ridiculed, humiliated, or rejected. Thus, the conscious experience of shame is more often associated with the idea of the external shaming object. However, the subject-as-agent in the shame experience is also identified with this shaming other. This "sadonarcissistic identification with the shamer" (Rothstein, 1984) gives the experience its internal quality. The subject-as-agent, the "I", is ashamed of the subject-as-object, the "me" (Rothstein, 1988). If the subject were to express this aspect of the experience of shame, he or she might say, "*I am ashamed of my*self." From this perspective, shame, humiliation, and mortification are conceived of as related synonymously. The content of each affect connotes a sense of inner disapproval, self-loathing, and disgust in relation to a fantasied other. The fantasied other may be experienced in various states of integration: within oneself or externalized on to another. Humiliated and mortified subjects experience themselves like embarrassed individuals. They observe or reflect upon an aspect of themselves experienced as an object and feel that "*I*" am humiliated or "*I*" am mortified about myself.

All human beings have the potential to experience shame and guilt. In addition to hypothesized inherited potentials that are beyond analytic validation, selected subjects who are particularly shame-prone have had shaping experiences with parents who enjoyed shaming or humiliating them. In this regard, I (1984) noted that selected narcissistic personality disorders

> were repeatedly humiliated by their parents as children. Humiliation was more likely to occur when they failed to live up to their parents' narcissistically invested fantasies for them or when their existence challenged their parents' other narcissistically invested pursuits. In addition they were exposed to their parents' more general penchant for humiliating those who failed them. [p. 99]

In this chapter, guilt, shame, humiliation, mortification, and remorse are conceived as components of compromise formations. All these affects express ways people feel and/or fear disapproval. Shame expresses a fantasy of a particular kind of parental disapproval or loss of love as an expression of a punishment that is feared or is sensed to have occurred. When the punishment is feared, shame is anticipated and associated with anxiety, the specific ideational content of which depicts the manner in which the subjects fear being shamed. When the punishment is felt to have occurred, the sense of shame is associated with depressive affect involving the ideational expression of the manner in which the subjects feel they have been shamed. Subjects whose lives are dominated by shame depressive affect are often described as afflicted with disorders of self-esteem. In both shame anxiety and shame depressive affect, the content of the affect is shaped in part by real experiences from previous stages of life. These experiences and the subjects' responses to them, however, inevitably resonate and are interwoven with "the child's earliest impulses . . . tender and hostile, toward its parents and brothers and sisters" (Freud, 1909, p. 208). Thus, when shame is conceived of as one of the affects that contribute to the variety of punishment fantasies, it will be obvious that it is associated with a conscious or unconscious sense of having incurred parental disapproval for behaviour or fantasies associatively linked to childhood sexual conflicts.

Freud's (1923, 1926, 1940) and Brenner's (1982) descriptions of varieties of affects involved in superego functioning are, in contemporary terms, descriptions of aspects of fantasies of object relationships. The contents of these relationships concern the subjects' fears of parental disapproval, punishment, and loss of love.

Among the varieties of disapproval, punishment, and loss of love a wide range of possibilities can be found that are shaped in part by the individual's real experiences with parents and parental surrogates. The manner in which parents approved and disapproved, rewarded and punished, loved and hated, admired and humiliated, affirmed and shamed, attended to and ignored, their children contributes to the content of the affects an individual may experience.

It is not my intention to suggest that shame and guilt are identical, or that one affect is hegemonic over the other. Rather, I believe they share a common ideational content that is influenced profoundly by the individual's developmental experiences. Both refer to varieties of *parental disapproval*. It is from this perspective that I am stressing the advantages of thinking of the similarities between shame and guilt. Shame is an affect connected with one or more specific types of fantasies of parental disapproval. Many shame experiences are characterized by the ideational content of the calamity of loss of love, anxiety, and/or depressive affect. Some subjects experience fantasies of disapproval and feel unloved and unlovable. They suffer from a chronic sense of shame depressive affect characterized by a predominance of loss-of-love depressive affect. These affects are shaped in part by perceptions of parental disinterest or hostility. It is not uncommon for such subjects to assume responsibility for their parents' states of mind in order to maintain the narcissistically invested illusion that they can omnipotently undo them.

There are a number of clinical advantages in the analyses of adults that follow from emphasizing the similarities between shame and guilt. First, this vantage point suggests that the manifest content of a conflict involving shame is invariably overdetermined and associatively linked to other, less immediately obvious superego compromise formations that may involve any number of amalgams of the other calamities of childhood. From this perspective, shame is conceptualized as functioning in part to screen and defend against even more unpleasant affects involving experiences of the subject's personal responsibility for taboo drive derivatives. This point of view counteracts the mistaken tendency to separate conflicts categorically into sexual, Oedipal conflicts, which involve the calamity of castration, and non-sexual, pre-Oedipal conflicts, which involve the calamity of loss of love and/or loss of the object. Those who emphasize the distinctions between shame and guilt have tended to conceive of two separate types of pathogenesis: guilt as related to conflict concerning Oedipal drive derivatives and shame as resulting from the traumatic influence of early experience. The contributions of Adler (1926, pp. 6–7, 14), Alexander (1927, 1938, 1948, pp. 123, 127), Piers and Singer (1953), Grinker (1955, p. 253), Grunberger (1971, pp. 267, 269, 270), Kohut (1977), and two followers of Kohut, Broucek (1982) and Morrison (1984), reflect the latter conception of shame as related to traumatogenic conceptions of pathogenesis.

Second, none of the authors who stress the distinctions between pre-Oedipal and Oedipal conflicts and between shame and guilt, including Adler, Alexander, Piers and Singer, Erikson (1960), Jacobson (1964), and Kohut, ever seems to consider that manifest oral and/or anal content might be over-determined and might represent a displacement from phallic, Oedipal conflicts.

In contrast to these colleagues, there is a tradition that presages the thrust of this chapter, acknowledging the descriptive distinction between shame and guilt while emphasizing their over-determined nature and their relationship to infantile sexual conflict. Hartmann and Loewenstein's (1962, pp. 66–67) comments represent this point of view. In contrast to Jacobson (1964), who found much to agree with in Piers and Singer's *Shame and Guilt* (1953), Hartmann and Loewenstein criticized the book along lines similar to the point of view presented in this chapter.

The perspective I stress emphasizes that considering shame as separate from guilt may have the *effect* of allowing Oedipal conflicts to escape notice. The analyst who listens from a theoretical perspective that categorically separates these affects will have a tendency to be satisfied and stop analysing after a conflict concerning shame has been understood and interpreted on a pre-Oedipal level. This tendency is most clearly demonstrated in the contributions of the self psychologists. These colleagues consider restitution as their goal. In their analysis of shame, as in their work with "self-state" dreams, they consider that there are no further deepening associations to certain dreams and states of mind. For an analyst working from a perspective that stresses the interminability of conflict, there are always further deepening associations. Conceiving of shame and guilt as related affects of superego functioning helps an analyst maintain such an analytic perspective.

Finally, it is a common experience that analysands imagine their analysts' approval or disapproval concerning their fantasies and behaviour. Analysands may begin a session by speaking of their shame. In selected cases, the regression characteristic of analysis can accentuate this tendency. Analytic work with such people typically reveals associated, less manifest affects related to a complex of drive derivatives. The following clinical examples are presented to illustrate the common relationship between shame and guilt as well as a number of related fantasies and enactments involving a complex of drive derivatives, affects, defences, and superego elements. The analytic data are from two patients at different stages of their analyses. Although these patients would be considered different diagnostically, shame was a prominent aspect of the life experiences of each. The data emphasize that shame and guilt are related aspects of all patients' experiences. They may be found in patients with all diagnostic labels and at any stage of their analyses.

First patient

Mr W began his analysis as a twenty-four-year-old virgin in his final year of law school. He sought help because he was tortured by obsessional preoccupations concerning what people would think of him—that is, by shame anxiety—and by feelings of worthlessness associated with fantasies of what people thought of him—that is, by shame depressive affect.

In his relationships with women, he was preoccupied with concerns that he would offend them by his sexual overtures and was paralysed with guilt concerning prospective sexual experiences with women he did not intend to marry. He believed that if he pursued a woman sexually he would lose her as a friend and ultimately be left friendless. In the past, he had dated women who wished to remain chaste because of religious convictions. More recently, he had dated women who desired sex with him. He felt it was unfair to take advantage of them and broke off the relationships.

The data presented are from the first year of Mr W's analysis. He treated the analyst with great deference and respect, anticipating that the analyst would have specific answers to his questions. He behaved as if he expected the analyst to offer advice that would help him feel better. He often complained of not knowing who he really was and of being torn between who he felt he was and who he felt he should be. At times, these intensely painful episodes of self-doubt and shame depressive affect resulted in disavowal of aspects of himself and depersonalization.

Vignettes are presented from two sessions during a six-week period of intense study for his bar examination. In my work with Mr W, I had come to understand him as a man who was extremely intolerant of any personal desires and as a very guilty person who was ashamed of anyone's knowing that he had a selfish, sexual, or hostile wish. He diminished his sense of guilt for these wishes by attempting to be the perfect "good boy" and was ashamed of any imperfection.

> Mr. W began a session by asking if I remembered what he talked about in the previous hour. After about five minutes of silence, I interpreted his wish for me to "get him started" as reflecting his wish to have me

take care of him and, more specifically, his desire that I share respon-sibility with him for his taboo wishes. In response to the interpretation, he remembered that he had been talking about a severe headache he had experienced in response to a conversation in which his successor on the law school curriculum committee complained about the curricu-lum. His associations shifted to the awards given to classmates for community service. He expressed rage at the awards committee for giving the prizes to people less worthy than he. He rationalized his rage and envy of them as well as his own inhibitions in pursuing the awards for himself. I interpreted, "You envy the victors their pleasure and success. You feel it is a sin and a crime to have any personal desires." Later in the hour, I responded to his disavowal of personal wishes. I interpreted, "All human beings have competitive wishes; all people want to win one thing or another. You feel that only altruistic desires are worthwhile and acceptable."

A few weeks later, Mr W began a session by relating that as he studied for the bar exam he was preoccupied by thoughts of failing and of being publicly humiliated. I interpreted, "You feel the need to shame yourself. You turn your exam into a drama of public humiliation." Mr W responded, "It's better than having it sprung on you. The best thing is to think you're going to fail and to do well. The worst thing is to think you're going to do well and to do poorly." I added, "To be surprised." Mr W said, "Yes. I'm not spending most of my time think-ing of failing. Rather I'm thinking of the sexual pleasure I might have in the future with Miriam."

In confirmation of Yorke and colleagues' (1990) view that "the roots of shame" are "in a regressive loss of sphincter control or its psychologi-cal equivalent . . . in terms of loss of attainments" (p. 404), Mr W's asso-ciations shifted to bouts of diarrhoea he had experienced the previous evening, which had interfered with his ability to study. I commented, "It's sort of like your bowels are humiliating you." He responded, "I feel like they're nagging me." I asked, "What do you imagine they're saying?"

In response, his associations shifted from anal preoccupations to heterosexual concerns. He stated, "I picture people saying, 'I thought he was such an intelligent guy.' I picture Helda saying, 'Gee, Tom is such a loser. I'm glad I broke up with him.' She says that even though I broke up with her. I think of Harriet saying, 'Tom is such a mess, and I'm running with such a tough crowd.' I think of them saying, 'How could we pass and you fail?' "

I interpreted, "When you think about what people will say you think primarily in terms of what the women will say whom you have disappointed . . . failed with sexually." Mr W responded, "Yes, that's mostly what I think about, wanting a satisfying sexual relationship with a woman I have a good relationship with."

Second patient

Mr A, a middle-aged accountant, had a father who would humiliate his son whenever Mr A attempted to compete with him. Mr A interpreted this aspect of his father's behaviour as "telling me that he wanted his son to serve him, to be part of his audience and his harem." His father's behaviour was a shaping influence on the calamitous affects that characterize Mr A's conscience. This shaping influence contributed to Mr A's developing a character style of serving his father like a woman, limiting his own successful masculine strivings and humiliating himself. He was ashamed of this manifest style, but this shameful unpleasure was more tolerable than the terrifying anxiety that characterized the guilt associated with his latent murderous, competitive, positive Oedipal strivings. After four years of analysis, Mr A was more conscious of these currents and had become less masochistic.

Mr A began a session in the fifth year of his analysis by reporting that he woke up feeling depressed in response to thinking about the nature of his relationship with his wife. Mr A had experienced premature ejaculation and loss of his erection in a number of past relationships and currently, on occasion, in his sexual relationship with his wife. His wife is a successful businesswoman whom Mr A serves as accountant and helper—her "gal Friday". In addition, Mr A feels that his wife is sexually demanding, that he has to give her an orgasm to avoid her disapproval, rejection, and abandonment. Mr A associated, "Do I want to live this way, serving Margaret all the time and living off her success? I'm so ashamed of enjoying living off her money and through her success." His associations shifted to a story he had read about the life of a very talented woman who subordinated herself to the service of her famous husband. I interpreted, "You're ashamed about your pleasure in being taken care of like a wife." Mr A responded, "Yes, of being like a woman. In bed Margaret is almost always on top."

Previous work had helped Mr A understand the negative Oedipal gratifications in the choice of Margaret as his wife. Mr A had commented, "It is uncanny how like my father she is and how I subordinate myself to her as I did to him when he was alive." Mr A had married Margaret on the seventh anniversary of his father's death. In the next session, he began to grasp that Margaret helped him avoid the experience of similar conflicts in relation to me. In discussing the possibility of his missing an hour that he had asked me to reschedule, Mr A stated, "I'm so embarrassed at the idea of your changing the hour and my possibly missing it." I interpreted, "You're embarrassed at the idea of disappointing a man who is taking care of you. You're embarrassed by the idea that you feel like a woman in such a relationship and by the mixed feelings you feel toward me as a man taking care of you." The implicit sado-masochistic gratifications in his "mixed feelings" were not interpreted at this time. This shame, experienced in the transference, not only gratified his negative Oedipal longings but was intended to function defensively and disarm the analyst as male rival.

Mr A's sexual symptoms (premature ejaculation and loss of potency at ejaculation) had previously been understood as an expression of his anger towards his wife, as a humiliating punishment for the expression of these wishes, and as a defence in response to the unpleasure experienced in relation to competitive wishes toward his wife, his father, and his analyst. The manifest sexual symptoms and the related wish to be a woman were associated with shame depressive affect and linked to castration anxiety and guilt connected to his more concealed masculine competitive strivings.

A week after the vignette reported above, concerning Mr A's wish to be a woman, he described a sexual experience with his wife in which he brought her to an orgasm orally and then mounted her and lost his erection as he was about to ejaculate. In response, I interpreted, "A woman can give another woman an orgasm with her tongue. To mount Margaret, penetrate and satisfy her and yourself with your erect penis is to feel like a powerful man." Mr A responded, "My parents didn't want me to grow up and be happy. Margaret says she feels as if my father is in the bedroom with us. Sometimes after we make love I think of them." I interpreted, "You fear they'll disapprove of your potency with Margaret." Mr A responded emphatically, "Yes! They just wanted to parade me around and exhibit me to their friends. They wanted to show them I'm their good little boy."

Discussion

These clinical vignettes suggest the over-determined nature of shame as an affect and as one of the compromise formations that constitute the superego. They illustrate that shame is found along with guilt across the diagnostic spectrum and at all stages of analyses.

Mr W is diagnostically an excellent example of an obsessional character. His most prominent presenting affects were shame anxiety and shame depressive affect. The analytic data presented clearly demonstrate that shame functioned in part both to reinforce repression and to screen guilt concerning sexual and aggressive wishes. Mr W was ashamed of any imperfection, be it his manifest experience of his body as imperfect or any of the disavowed derivatives of his instinctual life. He felt profoundly ashamed of any personal desire other than altruistic aspirations. He imagined that if his appearance or behaviour could approach his ideal he would be lovable, mitigating any need to be selfish and vengeful.

In addition, Mr W's associations demonstrate an important relationship between fantasies of perfection, shame, and guilt. Mr W pursued fantasies of perfection in regard to his dress and physical appearance as well as in various aspects of his behaviour. When he was able to achieve the illusion of perfection, he felt lovable, and the unpleasure associated with their sense of shame was temporarily diminished. Analysis revealed that these pursuits of perfection and the associated shame-filled calamity of failure helped to defend against more repressed conflicts concerning sexual and aggressive drive derivatives. Considering shame and guilt as varieties of affects related to superego functioning reminds the analyst of this common relationship.

Mr A presented as cool and indifferent. He sought a consultation because his wife was unhappy with him. His functioning in the consultation highlighted his proclivity for provoking humiliating criticism while masking the sadistic and narcissistic gratifications implicit in his masochistic provocativeness. Because of this mix of features, Mr A closely resembled those patients Cooper (1977, unpublished) has described as masochistic–narcissistic characters. Analysis quickly revealed Mr A's shame in response to the masochistic aspects of his character style. These experiences gratified negative Oedipal desires and both screened and defended Mr A from guilt associated with his competitive, positive Oedipal wishes.

In conclusion, I emphasize that what shame and guilt have in common are ideas of parental disapproval. Shame may be conscious and/or unconscious and associated with anxiety and/or depressive affect. Conceiving of shame and guilt as compromise formations and as constituents of the superego reminds the analyst of the similarities and relationships between shame and guilt. In selected cases, shame may be the most manifest of these affects and may, in part, serve to screen guilt. Analysis will ultimately reveal its association with guilt and other derivatives of childhood sexual conflicts.

PART II
CLINICAL IMPLICATIONS

The seduction of money

Mr Y is a sixty-year-old, married, childless, wealthy retired lawyer. In the fifth year of his analysis, he began a session by announcing that he was rewriting his will and would like to make me beneficiary in the amount of $250,000. When I suggested that he elaborate upon this fantasy, Mr Y became annoyed. He told me that I had helped him a great deal and was one of the most important people in his life. He wished to make my old age a bit easier. In the ensuing sessions, Mr Y became aware that, in spite of the reality of his considerable wealth, his wish to make me a beneficiary in his will expressed certain unacknowledged concerns of his own. He was anxious about being alone and uncared for as he grew older, and wished I would never leave him and would instead take care of him.

Four months later, Mr Y brought to his session an article on therapeutic nurseries that appeared in the newspaper. He was very touched by the report of these preventative interventions with young children and their families and expressed his wish to help. Mr Y had lost his mother as the result of a postpartum psychosis when he was six years old. He was by nature very generous and philanthropic, and was moved by the article to think about how he might help develop these preventative services. Mr Y reflected on the facts that he was childless, had generously fulfilled his obligations to his alma mater, had millions of dollars to decide how to bequeath, and thought that nothing would be finer than to create a foundation to facilitate the development of these wonderful services. He related that there was no one whose judgement he respected more than mine. He wondered if I would consider being the administrator of such a foundation. As far as I could determine, Mr Y had no conscious knowledge of my long-standing interest in working with handicapped children. I was aware of the powerful countertransference temptation to accept this seemingly rational and morally acceptable impulse towards generosity. Nevertheless, its relationship to the earlier offer to be my benefactor was obvious. Further analysis eventually revealed more about its concealed intentions.

About a month later, Mr Y began a session by reporting: "While walking to the session, I had the thought that we could call the foundation the X–Rothstein foundation." He laughed and noted, "That way we would be united forever." This gratifying fantasy of union was particularly poignant for Mr Y, as it reflected, in part, his wish to repair the shockingly traumatic loss of his mother at the height of his Oedipal phase. Later in the session, he reported that he was thinking about termination and wondered if I would consider the idea of being put on a permanent retainer to ensure my availability at short notice if he felt the need for a session. In exploring this fantasy, we were able to analyse his mistrust and his fear that I would not be there for him, just as his mother had not been there for him after he was six years of age.

Some other data are noteworthy in regard to Mr Y's use of money, both as an expression of his transference love and as an attempt at seduction.

Mr Y sought psychotherapy for the first time at the age of thirty-seven when he was single, successful professionally, and deeply troubled by his homosexual proclivity. Although he found both men and women attractive, he confined consummated sexual experiences to bathroom encounters with men whom he considered beneath him socially. His abhorrence of a homosexual way of life influenced him to seek help. He worked in psychotherapy two or three times a week for fifteen years. The interpretative approach of his therapist emphasized Mr Y's masochism and its expression in the extratransference sphere of his life. Mr Y had no memory of their having worked on his childhood experiences in general, or on his Oedipal conflicts in particular. In addition, he could not remember exploring his feelings and/or fantasies concerning his analyst. The therapy was helpful to Mr Y in achieving his goal of marrying a woman and in obtaining moderate pleasure in sex with women. After Mr Y terminated, he visited his therapist yearly. On one such occasion, in response to Mr Y's complaints about his wife, his therapist suggested that Mr Y should accept his wife as she was; she would probably never change significantly. The therapist added that perhaps he ought to find another woman. This remark terrified Mr Y, who left feeling that his therapist had become quite successful and had lost interest in him. This thought influenced Mr Y to find another person to work with when he sought help for a second time.

During the second year of his analysis with me, Mr Y received a letter from his first therapist seeking a contribution to a fund to support a psychiatric foundation. Also of note was a dream, perhaps six months prior to the emergence of his fantasy of leaving me money, which foretold Mr Y's subsequent attempt to seduce his analyst with money. Mr Y reported,

> I'm being conducted through a bank. If I'm not the guest of honour, I'm clearly a very important participant. This bank was previously directed by Harold Quieter. I was very fond of him. [Mr Y associates, "When I think of Harold I think of you."] As I approached the entrance to the bank, there was a large billboard. I thought this is an odd display for the entrance to a bank. I thought that although it was hard to believe, Harold seemed to have a conflict of interest here.

Mr Y was silent for some time. I noted, "In the dream, Harold's integrity is doubted." Mr Y remarked tersely, "Money corrupts." I said, "It never corrupted you." Although the content of this intervention was ambiguous, my tone of voice emphasized the transference. Mr Y responded, "I can't believe I have even a subconscious thought that it would corrupt you." He paused and conjectured, "I suppose I have a need to make you larger than life."

At this point in the analysis, I conjectured that Mr Y was tempted to test my corruptibility both in response to his past

therapist's appeal for money and in response to residual homosexual impulses that seemed part of the latent fabric of the more
manifest maternal positive Oedipal transference.

Ten years after terminating his analysis, Mr Y developed a
terminal illness to which he subsequently succumbed. After being
diagnosed, he returned to treatment to work on his experience of
dying. In our last session, shortly before his death, he hugged me,
told me how grateful he was, and that he loved me. After his death,
I found myself having a recurrent daydream: a lawyer called to
inform me that Mr Y had, in fact, left me $250,000 in his will. This
daydream emphasizes the ubiquity of interminable conflict and
analysts' susceptibility to the seduction of money.

Discussion

In the seventy-odd years since Freud wrote his papers on technique, there have been many contributions to the literature on
technique and on the subject of transference–countertransference.
However, there is a striking paucity of discussions about the meanings of money in the transference–countertransference aspects of
the analytic situation. As I worked to understand my countertransference responses to Mr X's attempted seduction, I found that
Freud's (1915b) final paper on technique contained guidelines that
seemed as valid today as they were seventy years ago. In that
paper, Freud discussed male analysts' heterosexual conflicts in
working with women analysands who had fallen in love with them.

I am suggesting that the fantasied gratifications associated with
money may be as much a problem as those associated with sex. The
guidelines that Freud (1915b) proposed for "not giv[ing] up the
neutrality towards the patient, which we have acquired through
keeping the counter-transference in check" (p. 164) in relationship
to working with heterosexual material are pertinent to working
with the issues discussed in this chapter.

Some of the foundations of technique Freud established bear
repeating. First and foremost, "The welfare of the patient alone
should be the touchstone" (ibid., p. 161). Second, "The patient's
falling in love is induced by the analytic situation and is not to
be attributed to the charms of [the analyst's] own person" (ibid.,

pp. 160–161). Third, "Anything that interferes with the continuation of the treatment may be an expression of resistance" (*ibid.*, p. 162).

In a sense the task is simple, but it is far from easy. The offer of money in any form and for any reason should be regarded as a transference fantasy. Like any fantasy, it is an over-determined compromise formation that needs to be analysed. To do otherwise is to perpetuate a countertransference enactment.

The analyst's attitude towards the future, and particularly towards the post-analytic phase, is especially important in regard to the issue of money. Because of the analyst's narcissistic investments in his professional endeavours and institutions, he might be tempted to rationalize the feasibility of accepting contributions from an analysand after termination. In this regard, it is important to remember that the unconscious is timeless (Freud, 1915b), and that analyses are all, in a certain sense, interminable (Freud, 1937). Any other attitude may interfere with the analysis of an analysand's attempts at seduction with money.

I propose that the data presented suggest that analysands' active involvement in psychoanalytic foundations while they are simultaneously in ongoing analyses may limit their work in the analyses of transference. Furthermore, analysts' treating such activity as simply "grist to the mill" may be both self-serving and over-determined. It is important to remember that analysands are unlikely to understand the importance of resisting the enactment of their conscious wishes to be generous. An alternative to treating such requests as grist to the mill is to treat them solely as fantasies best understood as compromise formations. I emphasize that this technical approach offers the optimal possibility of analysing their over-determined unconscious determinants. Finally, I suggest that analysts can benefit from considering such temptations on the analyst's part in the same manner that they would consider the urge toward any possible boundary violation: as an indicator of the need for self-analysis and/or consultation with a colleague who is not affiliated with a psychoanalytic foundation.

Although some analysts suggest the appropriateness of soliciting and/or accepting contributions from former analysands, I think the analytic material presented here supports my contention that to do so has powerful transference implications. From the perspective of this chapter, such behaviour may reflect a countertransference enactment that is a potential interference in the analysand's independence and post-analytic self-analysis. In addition, such behaviour might interfere with the analysand's possible need to return to the analyst for further analysis.

CHAPTER SIX

On beginning analysis with patients who are reluctant to pay the analyst's fee

The purpose of this chapter is to demonstrate the value of the concept compromise formation in working with resistances to analysis. More specifically, I discuss some of the things an analyst can do to help a patient who is able but reluctant to pay the analyst's fee at the beginning of an analysis. I will review some of the pertinent literature on technique and then outline my own thinking about how to understand and interpret this reluctance so that the patient can then experience a standard psychoanalysis. Two cases in which the patients were able but reluctant to pay the analysts' fees will be presented and discussed. Modifications of the usual procedures in regard to fee helped these analysands to begin working in standard analytic situations. Although these cases were unusual, they serve to facilitate discussion of questions of technique, with particular reference to the analyst's functioning in the consultation and in the opening phase of analysis.

Glover is reputed to have said, "If you want to sleep well, choose your patients carefully." I suggest that if you want to be more successful in helping prospective analysands begin an analysis, it is worth reconsidering the practice of being choosy. Implicit in my perspective is a criticism of the pedagogic methodology of institute courses in selection and unanalysability; candidate analysts are taught to be selective, to be choosy, to exclude people from the opportunity to "try" analysis.

Freud was also choosy later in his career when he could afford to be. His suggestions about the selection of analysands and the beginning of treatment were written from the perspective of the successful founder of psychoanalysis who was deluged by affluent prospective patients, many of whom wanted to be analysts and could afford his eight dollar fee. In spite of the profound differences between Freud's situation and those of most contemporary psychoanalysts, the technical ideals he enunciated eighty years ago remain the foundation of the standard technique with regard to the parameters of the analytic situation and the rules for beginning a treatment.

Freud's comments on selection are complex. In 1905, as he reflected on his experience in founding psychoanalysis, he noted that many of his early analysands were quite impaired. Psychoanalytic therapy was created through and for the treatment of patients permanently unfit for existence, and its triumph has been that it has made a satisfactorily large number of these permanently *fit* for existence (1905b, p. 263).

In contrast, as he looked toward the future and his commitment to establishing psychoanalysis as the optimal form of psychotherapy for select patients, his recommendations concerning selection became more conservative. Freud (1905b) stated,

> One should look beyond the patient's illness and form an estimate of his whole personality; those patients who do not possess a reasonable degree of education and a fairly reliable character should be refused. It must not be forgotten that there are healthy people as well as unhealthy ones who are good for nothing in life, and that there is a temptation to ascribe to their illness everything that incapacitates them, if they show any sign of neurosis . . . [A]nalytic psychotherapy is not . . . the method applicable to people who are not driven to seek treatment by their own sufferings, but who submit to it only because they are forced to by the authority of relatives. [pp. 263–264]

It is worth remembering that these comments on selection were made at a time when Freud's understanding of symptoms and character were quite different from our understanding today. Nevertheless, the moralistic tone that implied that good people make good analysands still influences contemporary considerations on selection. Most scholars of Kohut trace the emergence of self psychology to his 1959 theoretical paper on empathy and introspection. Equally important was his explicit reaction to the kind of conservative moralistic thinking that characterizes Freud and mainstream psychoanalysis. It is noteworthy that Kohut's first paper on narcissism begins with a long introductory reaction against such "prejudice". Kohut (1966) stated:

> Although in theoretical discussions it will usually not be disputed that narcissism . . . is per se neither pathological nor obnoxious, there exists an understandable tendency to look at it with a negatively toned evaluation as soon as the field of theory is left. . . . I believe . . . that these views . . . are due to the improper intrusion of the altruistic value system of Western civilization. Whatever the reasons for them, *these value judgments exert a narrowing effect on clinical practice.* [pp. 243–244, italics added]

In regard to diagnostic evaluation in the service of selection, by 1913, Freud's clinical experience had taught him that diagnostic interviews were not very helpful in prognostic assessments of analysability. Instead, he recommended a one- to two-week trial of analysis in order to ferret out latent schizophrenics who might be presenting as obsessional or hysterical neurotics. Freud (1913) stated,

> . . . I have made it my habit, when I know little about a patient, only to take him on at first provisionally, for a period of one to two weeks. . . . No other kind of preliminary examination but this procedure is at our disposal; the most lengthy discussions and questionings in ordinary consultations would offer no substitute. This preliminary experiment, however, is itself the beginning of a psycho-analysis and *must conform to its rules* [pp. 123–124, italics added]

Freud continued, "There are also diagnostic reasons for beginning the treatment with a trial period of this sort. . . . Often enough, when one sees a neurosis . . . it may be a preliminary stage of . . . dementia praecox . . . [p. 124]

Freud concluded these thoughts about the value of a trial of analysis by adding that if the psychoanalyst makes a mistake in selection, "he has been responsible for wasted expenditure and has discredited his method of treatment" (*ibid.*).

On the basis of these statements about selection and differential diagnosis, it seems reasonable to suggest that although Freud was undoubtedly interested in helping people, he was also motivated by his interest in promoting the field he had created. From his unusual and complicated vantage point, he assimilated his clinical experience with a group of prospective analysands. From this experience he wrote in an authoritative manner about the rules for "beginning the treatment" (*ibid.*, p. 123). He stated, "In regard to time, I adhere strictly to the principle of leasing a definite hour. Each patient is allotted a particular hour of my available working day" (*ibid.*, p. 126). In regard to payment, he added, "it [i.e., the hour] belongs to him and he is liable for it, even if he does not make use of it" (p. 126). In addition, he stated that he "also refrain[s] from giving treatment free, and make[s] no exceptions to this. . . . Free treatment enormously increases some of a neurotic's resistance" (p. 132). He did not comment directly on the advisability of reducing or deferring payment of fees. In this paper, I present analytic data to suggest that although Freud may have been correct about some patients, he was not correct about all patients. Fees have been significantly reduced for candidates since the inception of the institution of training analyses, a practice generally accepted as not rendering all such analytic relationships permanently distorted and unworkable.

It is a tribute to Freud's genius that although he stated clear and simple authoritative rules, he also communicated his profound appreciation of the complexity and individuality of each analytic collaboration. In that regard Freud (1913) noted, "I think I am well-advised, however, to call these rules . . . recommendations and not claim any unconditional acceptance of them" (p. 123). He continued,

> The extraordinary diversity of the psychical constellations concerned, the plasticity of all mental processes and the wealth of determining factors oppose any mechanization of the technique; and they bring it about that a course of action that is as a rule

justified may at times prove ineffective, whilst one that is usually mistaken may once in a while lead to the desired end. [*ibid.*]

The last quotation resonates with a letter Freud wrote, fifteen years later, to Ferenczi concerning the tendency of his followers to ritualize his suggestions on technique:

> . . . my recommendations on technique . . . were essentially negative. I thought it most important to stress what one should not do, to point out the temptations that run counter to analysis. Almost everything one should do I left to tact. What I achieved thereby was that the Obedient submitted to these admonitions as if they were taboos and did not notice their elasticity. They would have had to be revised someday, but without setting aside the obligations. [Grubrich-Simitis, 1986, p. 271]

In 1941, Fenichel began and ended his classic *Problems of Psychoanalytic Technique* by noting,

> The psychoanalytic literature is very extensive. It is amazing how small a proportion of it is devoted to psychoanalytic technique and how much less to the theory of technique: an explanation of *what the analyst does* in psychoanalysis. [p. 98, italics added]

To set the stage for my own considerations on technique with reluctant patients, I will outline relevant comments on technique from Fenichel (1941) and from two other classics on the subject, Glover's (1955) *The Technique of Psychoanalysis* and Brenner's (1976) *Psychoanalytic Technique and Psychic Conflict*. In doing so, two facts seem clear. First, Fenichel's observation on the sparseness of the literature on technique is as true today as it was a half century ago. The literature on technique concerning the beginning of analyses is particularly sparse, while papers on fee reduction are rare indeed. Second, the literature on technique is concerned with patients who are in analysis. In this paper, as well as in previous communications concerning patients' reluctance or immediate unsuitability to begin an analysis, I am writing about people who, according to our usual way of thinking, are not in analysis because they have not agreed to work with the analyst in the prescribed manner. If patients will not accept the analyst's fee, four or five regular sessions per week, and the use of the couch, such patients are thought of as not in analysis. If these patients are seen less frequently and/or work sitting face to face with the analyst, they are considered to be *in* psychotherapy, a psychotherapy that might aim, covertly or overtly, implicitly or explicitly, to prepare a patient to begin to be in an analysis. Such therapies must be *converted* into psychoanalyses.

Even though Glover's book was published in 1955, his comments on the opening phase were fundamentally those he originally presented as lectures to candidates in 1928. It is important to emphasize that Glover, like Freud, was writing primarily for inexperienced colleagues. In regard to selection, Glover, in contrast to Freud, believed he could select good cases in a diagnostic interview situation. He referred to such analysands as "accessible cases" (p. 186). Glover distinguished these good cases from "moderately accessible and intractable cases" (p. 187). He stated: "A prerequisite of successful practice is accuracy in estimating *accessibility*, or, to use a more illuminating phrase, the transference potential of the patient" (p. 185). Once the analyst succeeded in selecting an "accessible" patient, the opening phase with such a patient in analysis was conceived of as the analyst's "get[ting] the analytic situation going, . . . remov[ing] obstacles from the progress of association" (p. 38).

Glover's suggestions to his students reflected his expectation that, in order for a patient to be ready to be *in* analysis, a significant capacity for compliant co-operation must be manifest. Because cases were selected for candidates, Glover (1955) suggested that the candidate has

> first, *to confirm the patient's conscious readiness to be analyzed* and second to settle the various practical details that are essential to its smooth conduct. . . . The list includes: number of sessions per week, length of session, the question of a fixed or varying hour of attendance, number and duration of holiday breaks, fees, method and time of payment [and] the problem of . . . canceled sessions. . . . *On these and similar points it is well to have a settled policy and to leave the patient no doubt regarding it.* [p. 19, italics added]

More specifically, in regard to the issue of setting the fee and the related issue of the analyst's wish to make money by doing more lucrative, shorter, less intense psychotherapy, Glover suggested that the analyst ask "at what point must the legitimate economic motives of the analyst be restricted by his desire to practice psycho-analysis proper" (p. 20). Glover proposed that in regard to fee,

> there are two sets of sometimes conflicting interests, his own and those of the patient, and in the majority of cases the out-come must again be a compromise. One guiding rule should invariably be followed, namely, never to insist on a fee that is likely to be burdensome to the patient. It is generally agreed that a certain amount of financial sacrifice is favorable to the progress of analysis. On the other hand many patients in their eagerness to obtain treatment are ready to agree to undertake financial obligations that are excessive. [p. 22]

Glover is explicitly suggesting that "a certain amount of financial sacrifice" is also "favorable to the progress" of an analyst's career and the development of his or her analytic practice.

Fenichel's (1941) contribution was similar to Freud's in content and spirit. He presented the established idealized conception of technique as well as a more realistic appreciation for the creative possibility of each analytic collaboration. From the former perspective he stated, "The ideal analytic technique consists in the analyst's doing nothing other than interpreting, and the ideal handling of the transference too, consists in not letting oneself be seduced into anything else" (p. 87).

From the latter perspective, and in the spirit of this chapter, he noted,

> . . . we can and must be *elastic* [italics in original] in the application of all technical rules. Everything is permissible, *if only one knows why. Not external measures, but the management of resistance and transference is the criterion for estimating whether a procedure is analysis or not.* [pp. 23–24, italics added]

He continued, in regard to a patient's reluctance to use the couch,

> As a rule, we do not yield to resistances but analyze them. However there are exceptions to this rule. . . . If we have the impression that a patient *cannot* lie down and would rather forego the analysis than do so, we will allow him to sit. [p. 24]

Brenner (1976), writing about patients in analysis, noted,

> An essential part of an analyst's task is to understand the nature
> and origins of his patients' pathogenic mental conflicts. A consis-
> tent focus on this task . . . [a]s far as possible . . . should determine an
> analyst's behavior in the analytic situation. [p. 33, italics added]

Brenner's description of his work with a woman who was reluctant to use the couch is resonant with my description of beginning
with reluctant patients. Brenner described

> a patient who at the very start made it a condition of her treatment
> that she not be required to lie down on the couch. When asked her
> thoughts about the request, she replied that she'd been told that one
> of the things about psychoanalysis is that every patient has to fall
> in love with her analyst. . . . I said . . . "I guess you think that if you
> agree to lie down it's the same as agreeing to fall in love." No more
> had to be said. She walked to the couch and lay down like any other
> patient. [p. 181]

Brenner continued,

> Should one not consider that what went on during the few minutes
> while the patient was sitting in a chair facing me was analysis? . . .
> It seems to me very hard to deny the name "analysis" to what went
> on while we were face to face. [pp. 181–182]

Before outlining my perspective on beginning with reluctant
patients, I think it is worth reiterating that Freud (1913, 1915b)
was strict and authoritarian in outlining his rules of technique so
that neophyte analysts would be protected against the temptation
to be seduced into making suggestions, into playing "the part of
prophet" (1923, p. 50, n.), or worse, into the enactment of sexual and
other boundary violations.

I am suggesting that the theoretical perspective I outline can
help transform patients who are reluctant to accept one or more of
the parameters of the standard analytic situation into the more typical ambivalent analysands who work in standard analyses.

First, I approach a consultation with a prospective analysand
armed with the conviction that a trial of psychoanalysis is the optimal form of treatment for most people who seek analysts' help.

Second, in my view, a trial of analysis, of weeks to years in dura-
tion, is the most reliable way to assess the suitability for analysis of
a particular patient with a particular analyst. The trial of analysis is
conceived of as beginning when a patient first contacts an analyst.

Third, because assessment of analysability cannot be made accurately until an analysis is complete (see Bachrach, 1990), the analyst's focus during a consultation should be on analysing the
analysand's reluctance to accept the analyst's recommendation and
in collaboratively establishing an analytic situation. Freud (1913)
noted that the "patient's first . . . resistance . . . may betray a complex which governs his neurosis" (p. 138). Because that is true of
many reluctant patients, I have suggested conceiving of their reluctance as "enactment resistances" (Rothstein, 1990, p. 154). It is helpful, when working to analyse these resistances, for the analyst to
regard recurrent pessimistic thoughts about the patient's suitability
for analysis, and about the patient's diagnosis, as evoked or
induced *fantasies*. It is also helpful to think of the patient as analysable until the patient proves he or she is unanalysable in a trial of
analysis. Work to maintain these perspectives, combined with the
belief that analysis is the optimal treatment for the patient,
contributes an optimistic tone to the collaboration.

Fourth, in response to patients' reluctance to accept the recommendation, I begin by attempting to understand the resistance by
inquiring about it. I often ask, "How do you understand your reluctance to let yourself have the optimal treatment?" After making the
recommendation of analysis, I agree to work with patients on their
own terms if they accept that we will be attempting to understand
why they will not let themselves have the optimal treatment. If such
patients insist that they have absolutely no interest in psychoanalysis as a treatment but still express the desire to work with me less
intensively, I decline. I explain to the patients that they will be
better off working with someone less intensively who believes that
such a psychotherapy is the optimal treatment for them. A resident
in psychiatry sought my help and was adamant about his wish to
see me once a week. After experiencing his conviction about the
frequency he wished for himself, I asked him how frequently he
saw his psychotherapy patients. He answered spontaneously, "Two
or three times a week," and then added that he was in his third year
of his residency and there was the "realistic" possibility that he

might want to take a fellowship in another city at the completion of his residency. I made no comment about his concerns about the future, but thought about them as possibly part of *the complex of compromise formations that constituted his enactment resistance*. After a year of work with the reluctant resident, at a frequency of once a week, he was referred to a colleague for analysis at a fee the resident felt he could afford.

Considering patients' reluctance as "enactment resistances" reflects the evolution of analytic thinking about activity. Freud's (1914b) paper on remembering and repeating, written within the framework of the topographic model, influenced analysts to consider that enactments in the transference were undesirable and counter to the goal of verbally associating. Anna Freud (1968) and Boesky (1982, 1991) have made contributions that emphasize that activity in general and enactments in the transference in particular are fundamental to the understanding of a patient's conflicts. These contributions provide a framework that conceives of enactments, from a structural perspective, as derived from complexes of conscious and unconscious fantasies best conceived of as compromise formations. In this chapter, for tactical reasons, I am stressing the resistant or defensive aspect of the enactment.

Before I offer relevant clinical material, a qualifying note is indicated. I have presented a model for doing a consultation and for analysing prospective analysands' reluctance to accept the analyst's recommendation of analysis. This model is intended to counter the more common cautious practice of accepting patients' reluctance at face value, of working with such people in a psychotherapy conceived of as *preparatory*, and of overtly or covertly working to convert the psychotherapy into a psychoanalysis. My clinical experience continues to reinforce my belief that a trial of psychoanalysis is the best form of psychotherapy for most of the patients I see in consultation.

I do not recommend a trial of psychoanalysis to *all* the patients I evaluate. During the past year, I began differently with two patients who sought my help.

One, a married lawyer in her mid-thirties, was referred by her internist, who had prescribed Valium for the patient's first episode of acute anxiety. The episode had followed Ms D's first assignment as a senior associate after spending the previous four years in a "junior" position. The exigencies of her immediate situation required that she be helped to function on an assignment that had to be completed in four weeks. I understood her anxiety to reflect her conflicts over competition and success. Six psychotherapy sessions were sufficient to accomplish the goal of this brief treatment.

The second patient, a fifty-year-old virginal single woman, was referred for treatment after experiencing an acute psychotic confusional state that lasted thirty-six hours. Ms O was shaken by this unique experience and was very responsive to my interest in helping her. Because of the history and because of a subtle looseness of her associations, I proceeded more slowly and with caution. I began working with Ms O sitting up and at a frequency of three times per week. After a week, there was no longer evidence of disordered thinking. After a month, we increased the frequency of this face-to-face psychotherapy to five times per week. It is not yet clear whether this treatment will or should evolve into a psychoanalysis.

Clinical material

A number of years ago, when I considered myself "junior", a "senior" respected colleague called to refer a "good case" to me. I was quite pleased to receive the referral and immediately motivated to succeed with the patient, in part, to solidify the approval of this important colleague. After telling me of this "good case", my colleague added that the patient had experienced a failed five-year analysis and now required a reduced fee of $75 per session for the second try at analysis. I responded that I worked with a range of fees from $80 to $130 per session. I suggested that he refer the patient to me and allow me to work out the fee.

Mr A, a single academic in his early forties, sought analysis for difficulties in making a commitment to Phyllis, with whom he had been living for nine years. Previous analytic work had helped him to understand that his interest in affairs with other women and his terror at the prospect of the responsibilities associated with raising a family reflected personal conflicts that analysis might help him with. He believed his first analysis had failed because his analyst did not like or approve of him. He did not question the validity of this belief.

Because Mr A came seeking analysis, and because I accepted and agreed with the wisdom of the referring analyst's recommendations, our task in our first sessions focused primarily on negotiating the details of the analytic situation. Mr A's concerns focused on money. My senior colleague had originally referred Mr A to Dr J, who had stated that his $130 fee was not negotiable. Although Mr A felt he could afford the fee, he believed it was excessive and experienced Dr J as both rigid and arrogant. Mr A had told Dr J that he thought he was a "good" case. He added that because analysts were interested in doing analysis and because good cases were not easy to find, Dr J should be willing to treat him at a lower fee. Dr J's refusal to lower his fee had resulted in Mr A's return to the referring analyst for the name of a more agreeable analyst whom he might be able to manipulate.

After listening to this story, I said to Mr A that it was clear that money was important to him and if we could agree on the financial arrangements, we would want to understand more about what money meant to him. I added that I had a range of fees from $80 to $130 and that I would be willing to work with him at an $80 fee with the understanding that we would try to discover why it was so important to him not to pay my higher fee, despite his feeling that he could afford it. This arrangement was acceptable to him, and after two sessions we began an analysis at a frequency of four times per week. I add this note about frequency because subsequent experience with re-analysis has taught me to recommend a frequency of five times per week as optimal for "trials" of analyses after previous unsatisfactory analytic experiences.

Over the next five years, we learnt a good deal about the meanings of the modification that Mr A had insisted on our enacting together. The first thing he told me about was the shaping influence of his father on his attitudes towards money. Mr A's father had owned the equivalent of a motorized pushcart. When Mr A was a young child, the family business consisted of selling fruit from a truck in lower middle-class neighbourhoods. Mr A's father would cheat his customers by tampering with the scales that weighed the fruits and by "shortchanging" selected customers. Mr A recalled his father's pleasure in his experience of "screwing" his customers. Subsequently, his father's entrepreneurial ability allowed him to make a great deal of money in the wholesale fruit business, money Mr A had inherited and with which he did not want to part.

Thus, the first thing we learnt about his "enactment resistance" expressed in his concern about the fee was that he was enjoying "screwing" me rather than being "screwed" by me. Mr A was able to work productively with this insight and had associated to his belief that his previous analyst had interpreted sadistically. In this context, Mr A was able to work on his projective tendencies as well as on his competitive wishes to defeat his analysts. Over the course of the analysis, Mr A would deepen his appreciation of the complexity of his wish to "screw" me concerning the fee. He not only experienced interpretations as sadistic, but also as frightening, and he longed for anal penetrations. These frightening longings were related to his wish to be a woman, to have his father's baby, and to be impregnated by the analyst's omniscient interpretations. After seventeen months of work, during which time Mr A came to understand that he believed my lowering the fee reflected my particular interest and affection for him, he was able to voluntarily raise his fee to $130 per session.

A colleague described a similar situation. Dr T was working twice a week with a young married woman whom he thought should be in analysis. He had communicated this recommendation to her repeatedly. In spite of the fact that inherited wealth should have allowed her to afford the increased frequency, she insisted that she had discussed it with her husband, and they did not want to spend their money in that way at this time. At this point, in this psychoanalytically orientated psychotherapy, Dr T understood that the patient's reluctance reflected a specific identification with a penurious parent. However, attempts to interpret this identification and the derivative reluctance so as to be able to convert the psychotherapy into psychoanalysis were unsuccessful. The analyst believed the patient needed and could afford analysis. He also believed she would be better able to afford it in the future. For these reasons, and because he wanted to work in analysis with her, he proposed a modification to deal with her reluctance. He offered her an interest-free loan, and she accepted. He agreed to see her at a frequency of four times per week for the fee he was charging her for the twice weekly psychotherapy with the understanding that she would pay him the difference at a specified future date.

Discussion

It is important to emphasize that Dr T and I are aware that countertransference undoubtedly influenced our willingness to reduce
our fees for these select patients. This countertransference is understood to reflect an aspect of the match and must be attended to.
However, this countertransference may not be categorically different from the institutional countertransference towards candidates
that routinely encourages training analysts to reduce their fees. The
gratifications explicit in these countertransference–transference
enactments must be sufficiently analysed for analyses to be successful. I am emphasizing that, as with training analyses, reducing a fee
does not definitively distort the transference so as to render it
unanalysable. I am stressing that in all analyses, those conducted
with or without the analyst's conscious awareness of actively
engaging in gratifying modifications, an assessment of analysability cannot be made until the analyses are completed. Although we
do not as yet understand the fate of Dr T's decision to gratify his
patient, Dr T decided that he would not be able to learn about it
analytically unless he engaged in the enactment of gratifying his
patient.

For Freud and many of his contemporaries, "good" cases were
educated, worthwhile human beings. For Glover, good cases were
relatively compliant, co-operative human beings who could use the
analytic situation to express their transference potential in words.

Reluctant patients are not usually experienced as good patients.
They are often somewhat obstinate and/or defiant. They may
express some disdain for the analyst's preferred vision of the way
things should be, and they may present their own treatment plan in
an arrogant, entitled manner. A good deal of tolerance for this kind
of abuse, played out in the consultation, is required to help such
patients experience themselves as participants in an analytic collaboration.

In the examples presented in this chapter, I am emphasizing that
the *analysts decided to gratify their reluctant patients* in order to facilitate analysing their reluctance. This emphasis highlights the fact
that gratifying enactments are essential aspects of selected analyses.

Analytic technique has been taught from a theoretical perspective, which proposes that in an ideal analysis, the analyst functions

from a neutral perspective and interprets. At the same time, the analysand functions within the prescribed structure of analytic abstinence and assimilates interpretations in the service of analytic self-observations. This ideal analytic collaboration requires that the analysand accept the parameters of the analytic situation, including the use of the couch, a frequency of four or five times per week, and the analyst's fee. In addition, the ideal analysand is expected to possess a sufficiently developed personality, one that provides her or him with a reasonable degree of affect tolerance, a capacity to distinguish reality from fantasy, and an ability to observe her/himself. These traits are believed to be necessary attributes to enable the analysand to endure the regressive pull of the analytic experience and to resist diversionary enactments. Human beings who are not so endowed are considered unsuitable for standard psychoanalytic treatment. Some might be helped to become suitable with an experience of preparatory psychotherapy while others might be helped to have an analytic experience by modifying the ideal standard technique in the introductory phase of analysis.

In the tradition of Stone (1954) I have described modifications (Rothstein, 1990) that were helpful with analysands who were reluctant to accept the regular parameters of the analytic situation with regard to frequency of sessions and the requirement of regularly scheduled appointments. In that communication, I proposed that their reluctance could be conceived of as *"enactment resistances"* (p. 154) and, like any enactment, could best be understood as a compromise formation. I demonstrated that to analyse the enactment, the analyst must first be able and willing to accept it and to allow it to occur. I suggested that the

> analyst has to be able to accept that the patient must do it his way first before the enactment can be understood. Stated another way, the analyst has to be able to accept being frustrated by the patient while the patient is gratified. [*ibid.*]

In this communication, I am emphasizing *the activity* explicit in analysts' decisions to gratify their patients by treating them at lower fees or by offering interest-free loans. These patients' resistances to analysis expressed themselves primarily in terms of their reluctance to pay the analysts' fees. Traditional discussions of technique suggest that such reluctance should be worked with in a preparatory psychotherapy. When understood, analysable patients should be able to overcome their reluctance sufficiently so that they can then pay the analyst's fee and begin a standard psychoanalysis. In this chapter, I am emphasizing that for selected patients, the unconscious wishes underlying their reluctance must be gratified before the unconscious aspects of their resistances can be analysed.

The analyst's activity in gratifying these patients' resistances is conceived of as similar to the child analyst's agreement to play with the child patient. In the adult analytic processes described, the analysts decided that it was necessary to gratify their patients by playing with them, by enacting with them, in order to bring their transference potential, expressed as enactment resistances, under more focused analytic scrutiny. These clinical suggestions are similar to Stein's (1973) proposals with regard to the analysis of acting out; first the enactment occurs, and then, after the fact, the analyst works to understand it with the acting-out analysand.

There is an "established wisdom" associated with the ideal conception of analysis that suggests such gratifying enactments on the part of analysts establish unanalysable situations. I agree that it is better and possibly easier if an analysis is conducted without modifications. Analytic candidates are taught from a perspective that encourages them to believe that they can choose people who can be analysed without modifications of technique. However, the realities of practice confront neophyte analysts with the stark fact that many of the patients who might become analytic collaborators require modifications. My difference with the "established wisdom" is a difference of emphasis. I suggest that the modifications I am describing allow some patients to have analyses who would otherwise be unable to allow themselves such experiences. In addition, although I agree that the modifications I describe complicate the subsequent process, they do not doom these analyses to failure. These modifications are the opening expression of the transference–countertransference engagement that can be understood and interpreted in selected analytic collaborations.

In conclusion, it is necessary to discuss analysts' attitudes about the income they would like to earn. We are all professionals who have matured expecting to make substantial incomes. Yet, colleagues everywhere are complaining about the paucity of suitable patients who can afford to pay the fee the analyst expects or would enjoy receiving for services. In this regard, Glover (1955, p. 120), long ago in the mythical heyday of psychoanalysis, suggested that analysts acknowledge to themselves the conflicts and compromises required to have an analytic practice. He explicitly encouraged colleagues to "restrict" their incomes in order to have analytic practices. Such advice is undoubtedly easier to give than to implement. In a related vein, Erle (1993) has meaningfully discussed analysts' attitudes toward fee.

In addition to the conflicts just mentioned, however, analysts who believe that analysis is the optimal treatment for most patients are presented with an *ethical dilemma* when they have numerous open hours and are consulted by a patient whom they believe can only afford to purchase one or at most two of their hours. Do they refer the patient for the treatment they believe is optimal to a colleague who will see the patient in analysis at a significantly lower fee, or do they fill one of their open hours? I believe that if an analyst thinks a trial of analysis is the best treatment for the consulting patient, then the analyst will resolve this conflict by lowering his or her fee or by referring the patient to a colleague who works for lower fees, or to a clinic.

In this chapter I have focused on patients whose reluctance to pay the analyst's fee was a presenting resistance that required gratification before it could be analysed. There are, of course, many patients who are reluctant to pay the analyst's fee because they truly cannot afford it. When this is understood to be the case, the analyst will either lower the fee or the analyst will refer the prospective analysand to another colleague or a clinic. However, things are sometimes more complicated. There are patients who appear in consultation to be unable to afford the analyst's fee but who subsequently turn out to have been able to afford more than was at first apparent. Insurance policies that were not well understood, trust funds, or family support may subsequently make their appearance.

CHAPTER SEVEN

On diagnosing

The goals of this chapter are to demonstrate the value of the concept compromise formation in thinking about diagnosing and diagnoses as well as to explore the therapeutic value of thinking about psychoanalytic diagnoses as co-constructions. I will pursue this goal by presenting analytic data from a long re-analysis, and then by discussing it in the service of highlighting the subjectivity of the analytic activity of diagnosing.

My analytic work is organized from the perspective of compromise formation theory. This perspective emphasizes that analysands' and analysts' conscious fantasies and behaviours are manifest contents derived from complexes of compromise formations that are co-constructions. Compromise formation theory provides the analyst with a theoretical perspective delineating the multiple determinants of clinical data. An analyst working from this perspective may choose to interpret pleasurable aspects of data, unpleasures and related defensive functions, and/or their self-defeating characteristics. The dialectical–constructivist dimension (Hoffman, 1998) elaborates the reciprocal shaping influences of analyst and analysand on their respective complexes of compromise formations. I wish to acknowledge that, in addition to the important work of Hoffman, my thinking has also been significantly influenced by the contributions of Aron (1996), Gill (1994), Jacobs (1986, 1991), Levenson (1983), Renik (1993), and Stolorow (1995). This list is not intended to be exhaustive. Rather, it represents those colleagues to whom I have been exposed at professional meetings and in the literature, and whose work, to a greater or lesser degree, represents a paradigm shift in psychoanalysis that has been progressing for more than twenty years.

Clinical vignette

Mr X sought consultation with me four months after the termination of a seven-year analysis with Dr N. After hearing the patient's story, my impression was that his analysis had been prematurely interrupted, an event that had occurred in part, I conjectured, as the result of a countertransference response to Mr X's depressive affect and intransigent hostility. I felt it would be optimal if he could work out these issues with his first analyst. Dr N was someone whose work I knew had been profoundly influenced by Kernberg's (1975) contributions. I naïvely thought I might be able to help him resume his work with Mr X, and, with the patient's permission, I called Dr N and shared my impression. The analyst responded with the comment that Mr X was a "severe borderline".

Some time later, Mr X reported that he had attempted unsuccessfully to resume his analysis with Dr N, and again requested to begin a second analysis with me. In spite of his wish to do so, I felt that he was still too involved with his first analyst for that to be a wise undertaking. I told Mr X that because of his disturbed state, it would be best that he wait a year before making the decision to initiate a second analysis. (In retrospect, I conjecture that the disturbing nature of my response to Mr X had influenced my judgement.) At any rate, fifteen months later, he began a second trial of analysis with me.

Although Mr X was depressed and enraged, his capacities for work and for sustained relationships were impressive. He was a successful lawyer practising in a subspeciality in which he was quite accomplished, and he had friendships that had originated in childhood and deepened in the ensuing years.

The patient had married impulsively during the summer inter-ruption of the fourth year of his previous analysis. Although I conjecture that Dr N saw this impulsivity as another sign of Mr X's "severe borderline personality organization", the patient and I came to understand this event as an enactment motivated by Mr X's wish to diminish his unpleasure about, and awareness of, his homosexual longing for Dr N. These longings were intensified by Mr X's sense of Dr N's rejection of him. It seemed clear to me that Dr N had had enough of the patient's depressed, enraged longings and was glad to be rid of him. Here, I am emphasizing that it was not solely Mr X's symptomatology that was determinative, but also the analyst's reaction to it.

> Mr X began the first session of his reanalysis by stating, "For the last two years, I felt I was slapped in the face by Dr N, and I was angry. But for the past two weeks, I have been joyful, and I thought of kneeling next to you and stroking your chin to supplicate you. I had a dream: I was lying with a man and stroking his penis until he ejaculated, and then I was fucking a man in the ass. In the dream I had the sense that . . . 'Now I'm going to get mine,' as if I had been stroking Dr N, but now it's my turn."

> Somewhat later in the hour, Mr X remarked, "It's clear to me that I destroyed the analysis with Dr N by establishing rigid and stable patterns with him that put control on what I was feeling toward him." Later on, I suggested that he was worried that I would reject him as Dr N had, by concluding that he was too sick for analysis. I added that he was concerned that I would be frightened by his anger and by his sexual longings for me.

> He began the second session by stating, "I have a profound sense that you are really disgusted with me because I can't be analysed." He began the fourth session with ten minutes of silence, and then said, "I wish you'd say something." After pausing, he continued, "I have a sense of being blocked." I suggested that he was afraid his anger would seriously hurt me. He responded, "Just your saying that is such a relief. I thought I'd like to spit on your floor." To my response, "Only on my floor?", Mr X stated, "In your face. I'd like to knock you down and kick dirt all over you. I'd like to take a shotgun and point it in your face and pull the trigger and blow your brains all over the wall."

> I sighed and thought to myself, "And this is the first week of the analy-sis." A moment later, I recalled earlier work with a latency-age boy

who had shot me in the head with a rubber dart, and made the following comment to Mr X about his wish to shoot me: "That sounds like
great fun." Mr X roared with laughter, and remarked that he could not
remember ever having laughed with Dr N. Later in the hour, he
recalled his mother slapping him in the face in response to his com-
plaint that neither of his parents did much for him or with him. He
remarked, "My anger seems so vitriolic and bottomless. I get a real
sense of pleasure in being angry."

This experience of sharing his anger with me characterized a
good deal of the early analytic work. In addition to these interpretative experiences, which emphasized the pleasurable aspect of his
anger, a central interpretation of this period of the analysis concerned the defensive function of his rage: "It's easier to be mad than
sad." This perspective emphasizes the analysis of the defensive
relationship between Mr X's rage and his experience of depressive
affect. In spite of consistent interpretation, Mr X rigidly and tenaciously held on to his rage and related wishes for vengeance
throughout the early years of analysis.

Mr X began a session in the tenth year of the analysis by saying,
"Monday is Martin Luther King Day and I won't be here. When I say
that, I have the sense that to do so is an act of aggression. I'm not really
sure why. Coming down here this morning, I had the fantasy that I'd
announce in a flamboyant way, 'I'm here.' I saw a guy from South
America loading a truck in the cold, and I had the thought that I could
have a worse job. Then I had the feeling, 'You cannot hurt me. It
doesn't hurt.'" This sequence demonstrates anger employed to diminish the patient's unpleasant experience of sadness.

He continued, "How do I put these things together? Sometimes my
older brother would be flamboyant, and that would get a laugh out of
my mother. It was self-deprecating, but she laughed and that was what
counted. On some level, his behaviour acknowledged a fundamental
reality that my parents didn't want their children around; it was a forc-
ing of my brother and me on to them. So if, through the transference,
you are my parents and don't want me around, why does my not
coming here on Monday feel like an act of aggression?"

I replied, "You're doing to me what you feel I'm doing to you." Mr X
associated, "It brings to mind an adolescent memory. There was a little
cottage on my parents' property, and one summer, I furnished it and

moved there. It was as if I were saying, 'If you don't want me around, I won't be around.' My mother was livid. When I think of her anger, my reaction is 'So what, I don't care what you think.' Then I think, 'You can't hurt me; it doesn't hurt.'"

I interpreted, "Your anger protects you from feeling sad." After a silence, Mr X responded, "When I try to stay with that feeling for a moment, my response is to think, 'You can't humiliate me.' When I think of who she is and was, I work myself into a frenzy and think, 'It doesn't hurt me. You can't hurt me 'cause I'm the greatest.' I think of Mohammed Ali. All that is a complex way of keeping me from feeling sad about who she was and is. When I think it, I imagine being knocked down with no one to pick me up and dust me off. One reason it's so hard for me to let myself feel sad is that it would make my mother angry. No one else was sympathetic either. I would walk to the marshes to have privacy and to feel sad. I could also have privacy in the bathroom."

I interpreted, "You're afraid that if you're sad with me, I'll get angry and try to humiliate you." Mr X replied, "Were I to be sad here, I'd want to be comforted by you, and I know that's not the nature of the relationship. It's extremely hard for me to stay with that idea. There was no one who was sympathetic, whose shoulder I could cry on. I have a specific memory of my mother becoming enraged when I was sad with her. I'm not sure where that goes." I commented, "It goes into the pain of sadness," and Mr X responded, "It is a sense of melancholy I had in the marshes. The only memories I have of being overtly sad involve evoking anger and humiliation from my mother."

Some months later, Mr X began a Monday hour by stating, "I've been blue all weekend." He continued in relation to his parents, "I guess they're not the greatest parents." I interpreted, "You're struggling against accepting more definitively your feeling that they're lousy parents." He replied, "Sadness is like a garment that I'd like to throw off."

He was silent for a while, and then said, "I'm thinking of my father's office. It's like a castle and I'm looking up at it." His thoughts shifted to another childhood memory: "My friend Joey's home was on a lot of land. It was next to a gravel pit where people would practise their shooting and throw garbage. We liked to collect the gun cartridges, and I wasn't horrified by the garbage. I like old things, sort of like the garbage that reminds me of Mary's [his family's cook] kitchen and sitting at her flimsy old table, trying to maintain some dignity and pride, like a completely helpless newborn bird looking at the world with fierce eyes. My first impulse is to physically walk away from it. As I got older, that's what I did—I walked down to the marshes to be by myself."

After a pause, Mr X added, "And what? Being sent to the finest prep school is like eating in that old kitchen with Mary; it's the same kind of banishment." His thoughts shifted. "I'm thinking of playing basketball with my friends. My parents could be very friendly to my friends; they were warmer to strangers than to their own children. I want to say, 'Oh, God, none of this is possible. This isn't possible.' There is part of me that wants to say, 'I love my mother, I love my mother!' The answer is that she was who she was, and then I say that that's not fair. It's not fair that my love wasn't reciprocated. When I came home last night, Olivia [his one-year-old daughter] came to the door very glad to see me, expecting to be picked up and held. Who wouldn't want to do that? Then I think of saying, 'You can't hurt me.'"

The foregoing is an example of Mr X's momentarily angry, narcissistically invested defensive responses to his sadness. After a pause, he added, "That perception of my mother is something I physically want to remove. As an adult, I can mourn this, but that memory of sitting at the kitchen table is very vivid. The scar on my emotions is just as real as a physical scar."

About a month later, Mr X began a session by stating, "What I keep circling around and want to get away from is the heartbreak of the idea of my parents' disinterest and rejection. My first reaction is to think, 'You can't hurt me 'cause I'm the greatest.'" After a pause, he continued, "I had an image of standing in a foxhole and ducking down as a barrage of bullets were shot at me. Then I thought of my office at work and of what my new office will look like. The bottom line is that I don't like having my heart broken. When I say that, I keep thinking, 'You can't hurt me; it doesn't hurt.'"

Mr X's psychoanalytic experiences certainly do not demonstrate that his second analyst was smarter or more talented than his first. From my inevitably subjective theoretical vantage point, his experiences suggest that his first analyst had become used to diminishing the unpleasure he experienced in working with Mr X by employing the term "severe borderline" to express his frustration. This diagnosing activity on the part of the analyst highlights the existence of a common countertransference trend in response to patients who are experienced as difficult and disturbing. It suggests that there is value to thinking about psychoanalytic diagnoses as co-constructions.

Psychoanalytic diagnoses as co-constructions

What do I mean by this phrase? First, I wish to emphasize that there is a distinction between medical, psychiatric, and psychoanalytic diagnoses. Furthermore, diagnoses are nouns that are applied to subjects as if they exist as a fact of nature in another human being with whom the analyst is working. From a constructivist perspective, diagnosing is an activity in which the analyst is engaged in collaboration with, and/or in response to, another human being. Thus, diagnosing is a verb. I stress that psychoanalytic diagnoses are theory bound, and that various competing theories facilitate or interfere with the maintenance of an optimal analytic attitude. Some theories facilitate the analyst's urge to engage in the activity of diagnosing. Such activity may at times reflect a destructive countertransference enactment. Such sadistic diagnosing is often accompanied by pejorative labelling and by other potentially destructive evaluative activities, such as considerations of an analysand's analysability. The mining of this vantage point is the potential therapeutic value of this chapter.

It is important to remember that in medicine, diseases such as cancers and infections are tangible entities that exist in individuals. Although the aetiologies and treatments of many medical conditions are complex and over-determined, physicians are trained to discover specific aetiologies or pathogens that will enable them to develop specific treatments resulting in cures. From a derivative vantage point, physicians who specialize in psychopharmacology seek specific treatments for definable disease entities. Most psychopharmacologists espouse a bio-psychosocial model that acknowledges the over-determination of mental illnesses. However, many leading psychiatric researchers pursue strategies that seek to discover specific genetic and/or neurochemical abnormalities as the aetiologies of mental illnesses. These physicians hope that such discoveries will yield specific pharmacological treatments for diagnosable disease entities—that is, they conceptualize diagnosis as a noun. In fact, they may be correct for certain specific mental illnesses.

It is certainly true that most contemporary psychoanalysts, following Willick (1993), believe the development of schizophrenia to be powerfully influenced by genetic factors, and that this psychiatric diagnosis is a contraindication to analysis. In fact, a variety of psychiatric diagnoses are clearly indications for treatments other than analysis. However, as I have proposed (Rothstein, 1998), a trial of analysis is the optimal treatment for most patients who choose to seek an analyst's help.

Although many analysts are psychiatrists, it is important to remember that analysis is not a subspeciality of psychiatry; it is a profession unto itself to which people come from related professions. In that regard, analytic diagnoses derive from analytic work, and should aim to facilitate those interminable endeavours. Some diagnoses do just that, while others reflect potentially disruptive, destructive countertransference activity. I suggest that some of the difficulties experienced by analysts engaged in the activity of diagnosing derive from their conflation of competing psychiatric and psychoanalytic modes of thinking.

I view all analytic diagnoses as co-constructed fantasies understood as compromise formations. Diagnoses that facilitate analytic work represent normal compromise formations, that is, adaptive ones. Diagnoses that contribute to diverting, disrupting, and/or destroying analytic collaborations are pathological compromise formations, or maladaptive ones.

Such maladaptive diagnosing serves to diminish the analyst's unpleasure. Mr X's experience with Dr N emphasizes Dr N's hypothesized unpleasure in response to Mr X's sadism, as well as Mr X's depressed longings for loving closeness. The advantage of compromise formation theory for understanding countertransferential unpleasure is that it includes an appreciation of the complexity and over-determination of these phenomena. Although countertransferential sadism is a common response to patients who are experienced as difficult and disturbing, sexual desire and envy, as well as boredom and discomfort with the analysand's idealizing wishes (Kohut, 1971), are not uncommon, either.

An event in the fifth year of Mr X's first analysis demonstrates this point. Mr X announced his intention of changing professions:

going to medical school and becoming a psychiatrist. Mr X imagined that this would enable him to get a job in Dr N's institution and to work with him. Instead of understanding and interpreting the patient's intention to act as a fantasy, a manifestation of a negative Oedipal transference involving wishes to idealize, identify with, and love the analyst, Dr N responded by telling Mr X that even if he did become a psychiatrist, it was highly unlikely that he would be able to become his colleague.

It is important to keep in mind that practising analysts require a theory of the mind in order to function in the therapeutic situation. Until recently, it has been a characteristic of these theories to attribute failures to characteristics of patients' personalities and their diagnoses. The blame for therapeutic difficulties and failures has traditionally been placed squarely on patients' shoulders.

History of psychoanalytic diagnostics

In the following selective review of the history of psychoanalytic diagnosing and labelling, I will first present examples of pathologic compromise formations—diagnoses and labels employed to diminish countertransference unpleasure. Then I will explore examples of normal compromise formations—diagnoses that facilitate analytic work.

After a decade of pioneering clinical work, Freud created the diagnostic entity actual neuroses, and employed his first theory of anxiety to explain his treatment failures. An actual neurosis was understood to result from the conversion of undischarged sexual energy. Freud (1895b) conceived of such symptoms as "not further reducible by psychological analysis, nor amenable to psychotherapy" (p. 97). Because Freud was unable to understand these symptoms psychologically at this point, he judged them "unanalysable". Instead of considering his limited understanding as an operative factor, he proposed a non-analytic treatment: Patients suffering from an actual neurosis should be counselled concerning healthy sexual practices (i.e., "do not masturbate and/or practise coitus interruptus"). Eighteen years later, Freud (1913) ascribed his failed one- and two-week trials of analysis to the unanalysable subjects' affliction with "a preliminary stage of ... dementia praecox" (p. 124).

After a quarter of a century of clinical experience, Freud (1920) created the death instinct concept, in part to explain his failures with self-defeating, self-destructive patients. In his twilight years, he developed two concepts of instincts to explain treatment failures: adhesiveness of libido (1937, p. 241) and psychical inertia (*ibid.*, p. 242). Thus, Freud ended his career as it began, placing blame for the limited therapeutic efficacy of his discovery squarely on to his patients. This tradition continues to this day.

The diagnosis of borderline

The diagnosis "borderline" has an interesting and important history in analysis, elegantly chronicled by Abend, Porder, and Willick (1983). These authors emphasized that there is "a great deal of controversy as to precisely what the term means and how specif-ically it may be applied as a diagnostic construct" (p. 1). I will explore the history of the term selectively from my subjective vantage point, in an attempt to demonstrate that the diagnosis of borderline first appeared in response to particular kinds of frus-trating and disturbing analytic experiences.

While Freud (1937) was attributing treatment failures in part to hypothesized qualities of instincts, Stern (1938) suggested that we broaden our concept of a spectrum of psychopathology. In response to frustrating clinical experiences with patients whom he could not neatly fit into Freud's classifications of *neurosis* and *psychosis*, Stern created the diagnosis *borderline*. He stated,

> It is well known that a large group of patients fit frankly neither into the psychotic nor into the psychoneurotic group, and that the borderline group of patients is extremely difficult to handle effec-tively by any psychotherapeutic method. [p. 467]

Stern's paper is strikingly contemporary and well worth rereading. In response to the difficulty he experienced in helping these patients, he did what many subsequent contributors to the litera-ture on the subject have done: he suggested that their conditions derived from pre-Oedipal pathology rooted in disturbed mothering by troubled mothers, and advocated modifications of technique in the direction of supportive psychotherapy. Since then, a number of colleagues (Deutsch, 1942; Knight, 1953; Kohut, 1971) have employed the term borderline to categorize failed cases, considering these patients to be suffering from manifest characteristics that disguise underlying psychoses.

No contemporary analyst has had a more profound influence on the psychiatric and psychoanalytic diagnosing of borderlines than has Kernberg (1975). In part, this influence results from analysts' wishes to have a coherent theory that attributes treatment failures to their patients' characters. In addition, Kernberg's impact follows from his sheer productivity, as well as his talent and zeal in marketing ideas. He has been particularly successful in influencing psychiatric diagnosticians. Although the authors of *DSM-III-R* (1987) contended that all their diagnoses were purely descriptive and uninfluenced by theory, their description of borderline personality organization (pp. 346–347) was clearly shaped by Kernberg's writings.

Kernberg (1975) elaborated Stern's concepts from Kleinian and Jacobsonian theoretical perspectives. Like Stern, Kernberg experienced frustration and limited therapeutic results in working analytically with such patients. He laid the blame for these failures with the patients themselves, finding them lacking in many ways, particularly in the capacity to experience guilt, anxiety and depression. My reading of Kernberg is that he approached his patients with an evaluative attitude that was implicitly, if not explicitly, judgemental. He believed borderline patients employ primitive defences, while neurotic patients employ higher-order ones. He stated,

> Clinically, when we speak of patients with borderline personality organization, we refer to patients who present serious difficulties in their interpersonal relationships and some alteration of their experience of reality. . . . Such patients also present . . . chaotic coexistence of defenses and direct expression of primitive "id contents" in consciousness, a kind of pseudo-insight into their personality without real concern or awareness . . . a lack of clear identity and a lack of understanding in depth of other people. . . . They also show "nonspecific" manifestations of ego weakness . . . lack of impulse control, lack of anxiety tolerance, lack of subliminatory capacity. . . . *[This] represent[s] a general inadequacy of normal ego functions.* [1975, p. 162, italics added]

Kernberg's clinical descriptions highlighted both his interest in the psychiatric diagnostic schema of the *DSM* series, and the evaluative nature of his approach to patients. He went on to recount that

> In the hospital, I examined a college student, a single girl in her early twenties, with awkward and almost bizarre behavior, clinical childlike theatrical gestures, emotional outbursts, suicidal ideation, and breakdown in her social relations and scholastic achievements. Her initial diagnosis was hysterical personality. . . . I pointed out to her . . . the expression of deprecation of the interviewer, the effective avoidance of taking responsibility for herself by dissociating her concern for herself . . . behavior geared to force others to take care of her. . . . The final diagnosis was: infantile personality, with borderline features. [*ibid.*, p. 172]

Kernberg described another patient with whom "the entire interaction was filled with highly theoretical, philosophical considerations, and efforts to examine more personal, emotional material only intensified the abstract nature of the comments that followed" (*ibid.*, p. 172). He continued,

> I attempted to interpret to the patient the avoidance function of her theorizing. . . . As I confronted the patient with her defensive maneuvers, she became more disturbed, openly distrustful, and even more abstract . . . the diagnosis of schizophrenic reaction was eventually confirmed. [*ibid.*, pp. 172–173]

The tone of this last description emphasizes the possibility that the schizophrenic reaction was a co-constructed event. An individual's state of personality integration varies in response to the environment in which one finds oneself. Similarly, it is common for an analyst to experience a change in view of an analysand's diagnosis as treatment progresses. In response to the stress he encountered in attempting to help such "difficult" people, Kernberg recommended that analysts limit the number of borderline patients they work with at a given time. He considered it heroic to offer analysis to a patient whom he diagnosed as having "borderline personality organization".

In my reading of the literature, most theories concerning analysands diagnosed as borderline attribute the patient's difficulties to pre-Oedipally derived deficiency states that result in disturbing behaviours. These theories are often buttressed by selective readings of infant observation research. As noted, Kernberg drew heavily on the ideas of Melanie Klein and Edith Jacobson. Robbins (1983) employed Margaret Mahler's theories, while Modell (1988) applied Winnicott's concepts to explain the limits of analytic work with these patients.

Robbins (1983), responding to his only modest level of success with the difficult patients he diagnosed as "borderline" and "narcissistic", and dissatisfied with the theories of Kernberg and Kohut, developed a theory of his own to explain these problems. He drew on the observations and theoretical formulations of Mahler to propose a failure of the infant's ability to form a normal symbiotic relationship with the mother. He considered this fundamental to the genesis of the problems that he was unable to treat effectively in analysis. Like Kernberg, Robbins believed these patients to be lacking and unable to experience conflict. He labelled them *primitive personalities* who were afflicted with "a basic defect or developmental failure" (p. 131), and suggested that "the primitive personality *lacks* the positive substrate necessary to develop ambivalent dialogue with his . . . primary object'" (p. 145, italics added). Robbins believed this deficit to be responsible for "*a fundamental incapacity* to recall discrepant states and to experience simultaneously the poles of conflict" (p. 130, italics added). In addition, such patients "seem to *lack* the inner resources to be alone and self-contained" (p. 143, italics added).

Modell (1988), drawing on Winnicott's suggestions concerning early development, developed a theory of therapeutic action known as the *holding environment*. He stated, "The analyst's interventions are conjoined with the regularities of the therapeutic setup to create the illusion of a 'holding environment'" (p. 98). Modell attributed his clinical failures to deficiencies in his patients' personalities that compromised the ability to be "held". Modell's conception, however, lacked any consideration of the match between a particular analytic duo—that is, the analyst's contribution to the patient's capability of being held by the analyst. He wrote,

> There are patients who *lack* the capacity to make use of the illusion of transference . . . these people also demonstrate a relative

incapacity to process psychic pain. They seem *unable* to complete the process of mourning. [p. 101, italics added]

All these theories facilitate the frustrated analyst's withdrawal into an *evaluative* diagnostic mode, one that identifies defects and proposes non-analytic, supportive, and/or pharmacological treatment. Abend, Porder, and Willick (1983) provided a corrective contribution to the subject, emphasizing the role of shaping factors from pre-Oedipal, Oedipal, and post Oedipal stages of development, while stressing the value of interpretative analytic work with such patients.

It should be emphasized that when a cluster of clinical experiences accumulates that is beyond the capacity of the established paradigm to explain, it is not only because patients are difficult and/or disturbed. We must also consider that our understanding of these human beings may be limited.

Other examples of potentially maladaptive diagnosing

Kohut's (1977) creation of the diagnosis narcissistic behaviour disorder (p. 5) is another example of analysts' tendency to engage in the activity of diagnosing in order to reduce unpleasure in frustrating analytic experiences. Like the diagnosis *borderline*, this label represents self-serving diagnosing. *Narcissistic behaviour disorder* emphasizes the defensive function of Kohut's diagnosing activity. His earliest model of therapeutic action (1971), based on the notion that patients require help in recovering and experiencing the developmentally arrested, grandiose fantasies that motivate narcissistic transference phenomena, distinguished narcissistic personalities considered analysable from unanalysable borderlines or psychotics. This model proposed that if analysands were mirrored by their analysts and allowed to idealize them, their narcissism would resume its developmental progression. As Kohut worked with this model, he found that it was most effective with inhibited patients, while those who were enactment-prone were more difficult to help. He conceived of these latter patients as arrested at the stage of narcissism, and believed that their penchant for action contributed to their failed analyses.

Kohut's developmental model did not adequately explain his clinical difficulties, and we might speculate that it occurred to him that he could be facing a limit of his model or of his abilities. He did not seem to consider that the problem might—at least in some cases—be as much his own as his patients', or that he might be more comfortable working with inhibited patients. Instead, he resorted to diagnosing: he created the label narcissistic behaviour disorder (1977) to describe his failures with enactment-prone narcissistic patients. I conjecture that he experienced these individuals as more difficult and disturbing than inhibited narcissistic ones, whom he categorized as having narcissistic personality disorders (p. 51).

It is common for analysts to employ the adjectives *severe*, *primitive*, and/or *malignant* to complement the nouns that I have been discussing. These adjectives can also be understood as fantasies— as co-constructions created in part to reduce unpleasure in response to frustrating, disturbing patients. Dr N used the term *severe* to elaborate his experience of Mr X. Kernberg (1975) favoured the use of *primitive* and *lacking* when elaborating his characterizations of patients he considered borderline.

Bergler (1961) and Shengold (1994) employed the adjective *malignant* in a quite similar manner in describing their experiences with masochistic and envious patients, respectively. Bergler wrote extensively about the genetics and dynamics of masochism, having found that employing the above-described formulations was helpful with some patients and not with others. Instead of simply identifying the problem and acknowledging his lack of understanding, Bergler resorted to borrowing the term malignant from medicine for use in labelling his failures, together with the word schizoid. He wrote, "There exist two forms of *psychic masochism* which—though externally they may look alike—are completely different. [They] . . . are the *'neurotic'* variety and the *'malignant'* variety" (1961, p. 44). He continued, "'Malignant' psychic masochism, visible in schizoid and schizophrenic personalities, entirely loses the quality of an amiable 'game'. [These patients] are capable of a sudden, unexpected outburst of murderous rage, or of suicide" (p. 45). Furthermore, Bergler, like Freud, resorted to biological generalizations to explain the unexplainable, stating: "Probably the *biologically* conditioned amount of megalomania is different for every child" (p. 115, italics added).

Shengold (1994), in a manner quite similar to Bergler's, employed the adjective *malignant* to describe envy that he was unable to successfully analyse:

> Malignant envy is a retention of, or regression to, the original primal murderous affective mix. Clinically, one sees in malignant envy the phenomenon of the subject feeling with delusional intensity that what the envied one has is not only urgently wanted but has been stolen from the self—an intensity that is reacted to defensively by projection and delusion formation. This operates as a formidable resistance in analytic work. [p. 615]

Adaptive diagnosing

Before turning to a brief consideration of adaptive diagnosing—that is, diagnosing that facilitates analytic work—it is important to remember Brenner's (1982) comment that "the matter of setting the limits [between a normal and pathologic compromise formation] . . . is *an arbitrary one*" (p. 150, italics added). This comment reflects his implicit understanding that, although the diagnosis *pathologic compromise formation* is a noun, the analyst's conflicts and subjectivity influence his or her diagnosing activity.

I suggest two qualifications to Brenner's formulation. First, I caution that when the analysand finds him- or herself in too great a conflict with the analyst, or when the analytic candidate finds her- or himself in too great a conflict with the analytic supervisor and/ or institute, this state of affairs does not necessarily reflect solely the pathology of the analysand and/or candidate. It may instead reflect the inevitably subjective contributions of the analyst, the supervisor, and/or the institutional members or administrators.

In that regard, a determination that the patient's experience is pathological should not reside solely with the analyst. Such a decision should be a shared, co-constructed judgement. If a patient does not consider his or her experience a difficulty, then pathology is not present, even if the analyst finds the situation difficult and/or disturbing. Thus, when considering the shared experiences encountered in analytic work, it may be helpful to add the distinction of *syntonic vs. dystonic* to that of *normal vs. pathological* compromise formation.

It is clear that the urge to classify is a ubiquitous human characteristic. However, when I listen to neophyte analysts as well as to experienced colleagues present their work, it seems to me that they both employ diagnoses infrequently when the work is going well.

I have suggested that diagnoses that facilitate psychoanalytic work can be understood as adaptive fantasies and conceptualized as normal compromise formations. Accordingly, and with a view towards emphasizing both the analytic match and/or fit and my view that we human beings are all more similar than different, I have suggested that "prospective analysands can be grouped descriptively as (1) inhibited, (2) enactment prone, and (3) as too disturbed and disturbing for me" (Rothstein, 1998, p. 63).

Freud (1895b) labelled cases with which he was successful psychoneurotics. His earliest cases were hysterics treated with the cathartic method. Frau Emmy von N and Miss Lucy R's symptoms were relieved by relating them associatively to past memories and/or suppressed conflictual desires. Dora, Little Hans, the Rat Man, and the Wolf Man were psychoneurotics who were diagnosed as hysterical, phobic, obsessional, and infantile, respectively. Freud employed these terms to demonstrate the psychoanalytic method in general and its clinical application to the interpretation of dreams in particular. His descriptions of these cases highlighted Oedipal dynamics, defensive displacement, symbolization, and the concepts of ambivalence and anal regressive sadomasochism. Freud's portrayal of Dora, in particular, reflected his deepening interest in transference–countertransference experience.

"Some character types met with in psycho-analytic work" (Freud 1916) provided us with one of our most useful psychoanalytic diagnostic conceptions. This paper derived from a quarter of a century of clinical experience with patients, who, at times, seemed to Freud to be functioning "beyond the pleasure principle". Freud (1916) diagnosed three types of patients: the "exceptions" (p. 309), those "wrecked by success" (p. 316), and "criminals from a sense of guilt" (p. 332). Many of the patients he discussed were disturbing because they were enactment prone. Although this work heralded the introduction of Freud's final theoretical model (1923, 1926), his immediate purpose in describing these character types was to delineate a dynamic understanding of the unconscious fantasies that motivated these patients' disturbing and often self-defeating behaviour. Such understanding might enable analysts to formulate helpful interpretations.

More recently, Kohut and Wolf (1978) offered an elaborate diagnostic schema designed to help analysts analyse from the perspective of Kohut's revolutionary formulations of the narcissistic transferences and countertransferences. Kohut's schema proposed that a trial of analysis be conducted to assess the patient's capacity for experiencing coherent narcissistic transferences. Frank psychoses and many "borderline states" (p. 415) are vulnerable to fragmentation of the self and are therefore unanalysable, according to Kohut and Wolf. Analysable subjects, by contrast, can be categorized as "mirror-hungry personalities" (p. 421), "ideal-hungry personalities" (p. 421), "merger-hungry personalities" (p. 422), or "contact-shunning personalities" (p. 422). These diagnoses were proposed to help analysts more comfortably experience and understand these transference phenomena, in order to be able, ultimately, to communicate that understanding to patients.

In addition, in his effort to facilitate analytic work with narcissistic patients, Kohut (1971) emphasized the specific countertransference responses of boredom and premature disavowal of delegated idealization in response to mirror and idealizing transferences. Kohut's schema emphasized the analyst's ability to help the analysand feel understood, as well as to increase the analyst's understanding of him- or herself.

Summary and conclusions

In this chapter, I am emphasizing the unconscious determinants of all phenomena. Diagnoses are conceived as fantasies created by the analyst in response to another human being whom the analyst is motivated to diagnose. Analytic diagnoses, such as Freud's (1916) "criminals from a sense of guilt" (p. 332) and Kohut and Wolf's (1978) "mirror-hungry personality" (p. 421), emphasize various hypothesized psychodynamic formulations that are intended to facilitate the analyst's ability to interpret.

However, psychoanalytic diagnoses, such as borderline, narcissistic, perverse, psychopathic, and narcissistic behaviour disorder, do not emphasize formulations intended to be helpful to patients. Rather, they often derive from destructive countertransference trends. The analyst's activity of diagnosing and labelling the patient with such a designation is not infrequently a reflection of exasperation. Rather than saying, "I cannot analyse this patient," the analyst says, "The patient is an unanalysable borderline."

It is commonly accepted that analysts' personalities influence both their work and their selection of and/or attraction to the model(s) of the mind that shape and organize that work. My personality has undoubtedly influenced my pleasure in working with children and my attraction to Brenner's (1982, 1994) modernistic elaboration of Freud's (1923, 1926) final model. These experiences in turn inevitably influenced my spontaneous responses to Mr X.

A colleague who read of my work with Mr X asked how I understood the mode of therapeutic action of my playful remark in response to Mr X's expression of murderous sadism in the transference. This colleague enquired, "How does your remark, 'That sounds like great fun,' derive from your affiliation with and fealty to compromise formation theory?" I might begin my response by noting my belief that my personality contributes a shaping factor to the dynamic reorganization of my patients' personalities. Half a century ago, Stone (1954) emphasized the important contribution an analyst's personality makes to the modes of therapeutic action of psychoanalysis. He noted that "a therapist must be able to love a psychotic or a delinquent and be at least warmly interested in the borderline patient" (p. 592), and pointed out that "the therapist's personal tendencies may profoundly influence the indications and prognosis" (p. 593).

From the perspective of compromise formation theory, I stress that the analyst's personality contributes to the reorganization of those compromise formations that characterize successful analytic work. These transformations are usually described as structural changes. Arlow and Brenner (1990) stressed the role of interpretations and insight in their description of the mode of therapeutic actions of psychoanalysis, stating that

> what the analyst communicates to the analysand serves to destabilize the equilibrium of forces in conflict within the patient's mind.

> This leads to growing awareness and understanding on the part of
> analysands of the nature of their conflicts. [p. 680]

Thus, my personality and experience in working with children
contributed to the tone and playful quality of my response of "That
sounds like great fun."

Stressing the shaping influences of the analyst's personality—
his or her inevitable subjectivity—does not mean that the analyst
should not aspire to be neutral. Neutrality, following Anna Freud
(1936), refers to the analyst's unbiased attitude toward the contributions to the patient's conflicts of the three structures of the mind.
From a developmental perspective, Brenner (1982) emphasized the
shaping influences of subjects' object worlds, of their relationships,
on the development of their personalities. He stated that "a
patient's wish . . . has a uniquely personal history, a uniquely personal form, and a uniquely personal content" (p. 22). "Drive derivatives are substantially influenced by experience. . . . There is, in
other words, a more important relation between drives and ego
development than is usually realized" (p. 39).

These theoretical generalizations provide a frame of reference for
considering the impact of my communication to Mr X, "That sounds
like great fun," and the personality changes that characterized the
progress of his analysis. When I reflect on the beginning phase of my
work with him, I understand his sadistic rage to have been defiantly
organized in the service of vengeance, as well as the maintenance of
his sense of self and his existence—his very survival. This is what he
was referring to in his association to himself as "trying to maintain
some dignity and pride, like a completely helpless newborn bird
looking at the world with fierce eyes". And this is what I believe
Freud (1917a) meant when he noted that defiance reflects a "narcissistic clinging to anal eroticism" (p. 130). In that discussion, Freud
emphasized the shaping influence of the individual's childhood
relationship with parents in the genesis of the character trait of defiance. He observed that "Faeces are the infant's first gift [and] . . . as
a rule, infants do not dirty strangers" (ibid.).

I welcomed Mr X's vengeful sadism with acceptance, affirma-
tion, and trust in his progressive maturation. Compromise formation theory facilitated my appreciation of his rage as pleasurable,
that is, as a drive derivative. A fantasy sparked by my playful

response was internalized and helped to diminish the unpleasure that stemmed from his conflicted wishes. This process involved more than cognitive understanding; it involved Mr X's gradual acceptance and enjoyment of derivatives of his sadism in such personality features as a developing sense of humour.

My application of compromise formation theory also facilitated analysis of the complexity of Mr X's rage. Subsequent analytic work led to his understanding of its defensive function in reducing unpleasure, as well as its self-defeating nature. This work on the defensive functions of his rage, in conjunction with work on narcissistic and masochistic defences (see Chapters Two and Three), potentiated Mr X's experience of sadness in response to memories of parental abuse (maternal sadism, paternal disinterest and neglect, primal scene stimulation) and the limits of his power to obtain Oedipally organized gratifications. Analysis of the masochistic, self-defeating aspects of his rage helped Mr X to mourn his wish for vengeance in response to past injuries, and to focus on more adaptive here-and-now and future-orientated pleasures.

In contrast to my affirming, accepting, and trusting attitude, Dr N, strongly influenced by Kernberg's contributions, had responded to Mr X's manifest sadism with an evaluative, rejecting attitude that included labelling Mr X as a severe borderline. Dr N's attitude contributed a shaping factor to Mr X's first analysis that re-enacted Mr X's experience of his parents' rejection of him. It reinforced his fantasy that he was unlovable because he was enraged, sadistic, and murderously competitive. It intensified his self-esteem difficulties and the depressive tone that characterized his personality.

The diagnosis of severe borderline, with which Dr N labelled Mr X, was a co-construction created by both parties to a painful, frustrating, stalemated relationship. Similarly, Dr N's evaluation that Mr X presented only limited analysability was a self-serving one, in that it functioned to diminish the analyst's unpleasure in response to his sense of failure in working with this patient. The clinical material demonstrates that Mr X did not in fact lack the capacity to experience depression, which leads me to stress that descriptive phenomena should be viewed in the context of the manifest contents of patients' personalities.

In conclusion, I have emphasized that psychoanalytic diagnoses are creative co-constructions that emerge in the minds of analysts, and occasionally in those of sophisticated patients, in response to their shared experiences. They can be usefully thought of as fantasies—as compromise formations—rather than as purely objective disease entities.

CHAPTER EIGHT

The failure of an illusion

Many colleagues are dissatisfied and unhappy with their practices. Six hundred certified members of the American Psychoanalytic Association responded to a recent survey on practice. Twenty per cent had no cases in analysis. Most spent a majority of their time in clinical activities other than conducting analyses. For the most part, only training analysts had analytic practices.

About thirty years ago, a depressed colleague was bemoaning the state of his practice. When I told him I had ten cases in analysis, he responded, "That's because you are very published." I thought, "No, it is because I know something about helping patients begin their analyses." I decided to observe the way I did consultations and began analyses. This led to the publication of a number of scientific papers and a book.

In the process of discussing my findings, I became aware that the traditional pedagogy regarding selection, which has been employed for the past eighty years, had failed. Authoritative training analysts have propagated the illusion that prospective analysands could be *evaluated* in face-to-face consultation and that suitable good cases could be selected. The evaluative model proposes that analysts can "make an *objective* and *unbiased* evaluation" (Lagerwof & Segrell, 2003, p. 126) of a prospective analysand who is "suitable . . . for candidates . . . By 'suitable case' is meant a patient who is believed to be able to cooperate . . . with a good enough analyst in training and to complete the analysis".

The myth that an evaluation is possible in a consultation has been propagated in courses on "selection" and "analysability". These courses persist in spite of the fact that outcome research demonstrates that it is not possible to accurately prognosticate outcome at the beginning of analyses. Relatedly, many candidates begin analyses with patients who have been "chosen" and "approved" of by others. This process de-emphasizes the importance of "match" as a factor in outcome. Such a model proposes that the analyst, as authority, greet a prospective patient with an *evaluative* attitude. The analyst is trained to ask the question, "Is this patient analysable?" In an effort to answer that question, the analyst assesses the patient's personality and makes a diagnosis. If the patient is considered "neurotic", or, in Glover's (1955) terms, "transference accessible" (pp. 185–187), analysis is the recommended treatment. To begin an analysis, a patient must be ready to meet with the analyst four or five times a week and assume a supine position while attempting to put his experiences into words. Colleagues whose attitudes are influenced by an evaluative model seek compliant patients.

If the patient's personality is considered impaired or defective, or worse, if the patient receives one of the dreaded diagnoses, "borderline", "narcissistic", or, even worse, "psychopathic" or "paranoid", or if he is in the habit of using drugs, he is considered not ready at this time or unsuitable for analytic treatment. In such a situation, a treatment conceptualized as "psychotherapy" that is "less intensive", "preparatory", "ego strengthening", and/or "supportive" is recommended. In contemporary practice, an analyst working from an evaluative perspective might also recommend adjunctive psychopharmacological treatment. After a period of such treatment, a patient might seem more suitable for treatment with psychoanalysis. This requires that the *former* psychotherapy be *converted* to a psychoanalysis.

Results of recent studies reported from the Columbia University Center for Psychoanalytic Training and Research support my view that the evaluative model has failed and that patients are more likely to have successful analytic experiences if they are collaboratively developed rather than evaluated and assigned.

Caligor and colleagues (2009) described evaluations conducted by candidates supervised by training analysts. Their methodology attempted to make their evaluations as objective as possible. Prospective analysands participated in structured interviews and questionnaires as well as specific tests intended to quantitatively measure depression and anxiety. Employing these tests, as well as evaluations of ego functions, symptoms, and diagnoses, Caligor and colleagues found no differences between patients accepted and rejected for psychoanalysis. Reflecting on their findings, they suggested that "the criteria used to recommend analysis may simply reflect the perpetuation of unfounded myths about who would and who would not benefit from analytic treatment" (p. 690).

Hamilton, Wininger, and Roose reported that 40% of patients evaluated as analysable dropped out of analysis with candidates within the first year of treatment. Cases were more likely to fail (50%) if they were assigned rather than converted (29%) from candidates' psychotherapy practices. These findings support the idea that success is more likely if cases are collaboratively developed.

Before I outline my contrasting perspective, I emphasize that it is, of course, obvious that there are some patients (such as many of those described by Axis 1 diagnoses of *DSM-IV*) who would be better served by some other form of treatment than psychoanalysis (American Psychiatric Association, 1994). However, for the vast majority of patients, it is more a matter of the analyst's taste than of scientific clinical assessment.

The ideas presented here did not evolve in response to questions concerning analytic failures or hypothesized "deficits" in analysands' capacities. Rather, they are responses to the dissatisfaction many of my colleagues expressed regarding their practices. In response, I wondered why so many well-trained colleagues were having so much trouble developing and maintaining an analytic practice. In attempting to answer that question, I inadvertently stumbled upon a revolutionary (with a "small r") answer to the problem. I discovered in my attitudes and in my way of working in a consultation a new "concrete puzzle solution" (Kuhn, 1962,

p. 175) to the problem of how to help a prospective, often reluctant, collaborator give analysis a "try".

I call this new concrete puzzle solution a "trusting" model for doing a consultation and beginning an analysis. I trust that people who come seeking our help really *do* want our help. Regardless of their presenting complaints and/or deficiencies, which I regard as analogous to manifest content of dreams, I trust that they want to improve their lives. The analyst working from the perspective of the *trusting* model asks the question, "How can I help this person begin a trial of analysis with me at this time in our lives?"

I greet prospective analysands armed with the conviction that analysis is the optimal treatment for them. For an analyst to communicate such a belief, he must have conviction concerning the therapeutic efficacy of psychoanalysis. I optimistically trust that *we* will be successful in our collaborative enterprise. I assume that patients are analysable until they prove they are unanalysable in a trial analysis. Such a trial may last for as much as two to three years.

If such a trial fails, it does not mean that the patient is unanalysable. All I can say after such a failure is that *we* failed, that we were unable to collaborate successfully at this time in *our* lives. Such a patient might be analysable with another colleague, or might be analysable with me at another time in *our* lives. A judgement is made concerning the success or failure of the collaboration rather than of the analysand seen in isolation. If a trial of analysis fails, all we can say is that the analytic couple was not "collaborative".

The difference between recommending a trial of analysis and recommending analysis is frequently obfuscated and/or confused. Freud (1913) was clear about the distinction between recommending analysis and recommending a *trial* of analysis. He stated,

> I have made it my habit, when I know little about a patient, only to take him on at first provisionally, for a period of one to two weeks. . . . No other kind of preliminary examination but this procedure is at our disposal; the most lengthy discussions and questioning in ordinary consultations would offer no substitute. This preliminary experience, however, is itself the *beginning of a psychoanalysis* and must conform to its rules. [p. 124, italics added]

By contrast, recommending analysis "rather than a trial of analysis" derives from the evaluative model and a belief in the analyst's capacity to render an objective judgement. Recommending a trial of analysis derives from my belief that for most prospective analysands, the analyst cannot know, without a trial, with whom she/he can successfully collaborate. For this reason, I often say to a patient, "We can give it a try and we will know in three to six months if it is for you."

When a patient seeks a consultation with me, when a patient seeks my help, I am not particularly interested in evaluating his personality, and, relatedly, in diagnosing him. Instead, I am focused on helping him accept the recommendation of a trial of analysis as the optimal treatment for him. In that regard, I am interested in his sensitivities and responses to me and to the recommendation of analysis. The emphasis here is on the analyst's always working to restrict his functioning to analysing. From this perspective, the analyst's urge to evaluate, diagnose, prognosticate, and/or medicate, rather than to analyse, *may* be regarded as a possible countertransference signal. The analyst should regard recurrent pessimistic thoughts about a patient's suitability for analysis and his diagnosis as manifestations of evoked or induced fantasies. If I find myself thinking about differential diagnosis, rather than considering a patient's sensitivity, I consider that I am responding to some transference trend that evokes unpleasure in me. Countertransference unpleasure, associated with feelings of revulsion for a patient, may be defended against by distancing oneself in the process of considering the prospective analysand's diagnosis.

Some colleagues seem not only to misunderstand my suggestion that analysts' urge to diagnose *may* reflect countertransference; they seem to find it offensive. One colleague strongly objected to my emphasis on the possible relationship between the analyst's activity of diagnosing and countertransference difficulty with the assertion, "It is my professional responsibility to make a diagnosis. It is malpractice not to make a diagnosis." In elaborating a trusting model, I have proposed that colleagues "Consider that the urge to diagnose a patient *may* reflect a countertransference enactment", emphasizing the modifier "may", which derives from an analytic attitude that privileges countertransference. It is, of course, obvious that there are patients (such as many of those characterized by the Axis 1 diagnoses of *DSM-IV*) who would be better served by some other form of treatment (American Psychiatric Association, 1994).

The analyst cannot help being evaluative. I emphasize that it is more useful for the analyst to consider such urges as *possible* expressions of countertransference. From this perspective, it is best for him to concentrate his efforts on understanding a patient's reaction to the recommendation of a trial of analysis as the optimal treatment for him.

Analysts wear two hats; one is that of a psychoanalyst and the second that of a psychiatrist, psychologist, and/or social worker. In wearing the second cap, one will inevitably diagnose patients, particularly those with serious psychiatric diagnoses. Wearing the first cap, the collaborative pair will profit if the analyst considers that the urge to diagnose a patient as "borderline", "narcissistic", "infantile", and/or "sociopathic" may reflect a countertransference reaction. Such patients might be better served if they were diagnosed "too disturbed and disturbing for me".

If a patient objects to one or more of the parameters that define the analytic situation, such as frequency and/or the use of the couch, I agree to begin *analytic work* (I do not conceptualize this as psychotherapy) with the patient at any frequency the patient desires, with the understanding that an aspect of the work will be our effort to understand why he objects to a frequency of four to five times per week and/or the use of couch. I conceive of such objections as *enactment resistances*. In this discussion, I have emphasized my subjectivity and my analytic attitudes. In the context of doing a consultation and recommending a *trial* of analysis, it is the analyst's attitude, rather than the formal parameters of the analytic situation, that defines a collaboration as an analysis.

The prospective analysand's objections are viewed as enactments that are analogous to symptoms. The symptomatic enactments often have a transference significance and derive from unconscious fantasies that are best understood as compromise formations. The analyst has to be able to accept that the patient must do it his way first, before the enactment can be understood. Stated another way, the analyst has to be able to accept being frustrated by the patient while the patient is gratified.

An analytic attitude that accepts the patient's imperative desire for gratification as an aspect of a symptomatic enactment may engender a collaboration with the analysand so that his or her objections to accepting the analyst's recommendation can be understood as resistances. When these defensive aspects of the enactment are sufficiently understood as resistances, the analysand "if analysable with the particular analyst at this time in their lives" should be able to proceed with the analysis in the recommended manner.

In a sense, my approach frames the patient's reluctance as a self-defeating masochistic enactment and, in collaboration with the patient, focuses an aspect of the early work on understanding this expression of the neophyte analysand's character. It is not infrequent to find that this symptomatic expression of his or her character reflects the expression of more pervasive masochistic conflicts.

Reluctant patients are not usually experienced as "good" patients. They are often somewhat obstinate and defiant. They may express some disdain for the analyst's preferred vision of the way things should be, and present their own treatment plan in an arrogant and entitled manner. A good deal of tolerance for this kind of abuse, played out in the consultation, is required to help such patients experience themselves as participants in an analytic collaboration.

My perspective emphasizes that, particularly in a consultation and at the beginnings of an analysis, it is not primarily the parameters of the analytic situation that define a treatment as an *analysis*. It is the analyst's *attitude* toward the patient and the patient's behaviour and verbal associations that fundamentally define a treatment as a psychoanalysis. Other features of the analytic situation, such as frequency of sessions and the use of the couch, though important, are not always absolutely essential. I qualify this statement with my biased point of view that considers a trial of analysis to have failed if the standard parameters of the analytic situation are not established by the conclusion of the collaboration.

In summary, a trusting model encompasses the following six premises.

1. Analysis is the optimal therapy for *most* patients who seek your help.
2. Recommend a *trial* of analysis to most people you experience in a consultation.
3. Work to maintain a positive *attitude* toward the outcome of the trial. If you find yourself feeling pessimistic and/or experiencing an impasse and/or the urge to diagnose a patient, consider

the possibility that you *may* be having a negative countertrans-ference response.

4. Begin the trial in any way the patient is able to begin. The ulti-mate goal of the trial is to establish a collaboration at the frequency of four or five times per week and to use the couch. Think of the patient's reluctances to establish such a situation and to deprive him- or herself of the optimal treatment as *enactment resistances*.

5. Consider the patient analysable until he/she has proven unanalysable with you at this time in *your* lives.

6. Think of impasses and/or failures as failures in collaboration rather than reflections of patients' analysability.

If you accept the validity and usefulness of the trusting model, revision of analytic curricula is required. Because it is impossible to assess who is analysable at the beginning of an analysis, courses on selection should be deleted. In their place, a trusting model should be taught. This approach has pedagogic implications for teaching beginning phase process. In addition, a course could be offered that provides candidates an opportunity to discuss their psychotherapy practices. In this course, candidates could be helped to consider a number of questions: (1) why is not each of your psychotherapy patients engaged in a trial of analysis with you? (2) why are you not more optimistic about the therapeutic efficiency of psychoanalysis? (3) why don't you offer a trial of analysis to a wider range of patients?

In conclusion, I emphasize that the concept of "analysability" derives from the medical psychiatric tradition from which psycho-analysis originated. Freud, the neurologist, was interested in estab-lishing a diagnosis and in developing a specific treatment modality for the treatment of specific disease entities. I am suggesting that the trusting model reflects the evolution of psychoanalysis as a discipline in its own right. From this perspective, psychoanalysis is not a subspeciality of psychiatry, psychology, or social work. Its practitioners are not psychiatrists, psychologists, or social workers; they are psychoanalysts. As this perspective results in a different experience of ourselves, it also creates a different perspective on our analysands. There are no "good" or "bad" analysands; there are relatively successful trials of analysis and relatively unsuccessful trials of analysis.

Conclusion

This book makes explicit and emphasizes what is implicit in the contributions of Arlow (1969) and Brenner (1982, 1994): unconscious conflict is ubiquitous and interminable, all perceptions and thoughts are subjective, and all experiences in relationships are intersubjective.

The emphasis on the ubiquity and interminability of conflict stresses that there are no purely rational, mature, integrated thoughts or perceptions. All thoughts and perceptions are subjective. To the degree that the concept of neutrality implies the objectivity of the analyst, it is mythic. Arlow's (1969) delineation of the conflictual nature of thought and perception, and Brenner's (1982) description of the interminable irrationality of analyst and analysand as manifest in part in the transference and countertransference, delineates a ubiquitous subjective perspective.

In this conclusion, I am stressing the intersubjective dimension of compromise formation theory, which explicitly emphasizes that the intrapsychic conflicts of the analyst and analysand are continually and reciprocally experienced. These conflicts exert an ongoing, continual influence on their respective subjectivities. The four components of conflict are continually and reciprocally influenced, and, to some degree, shaped and reshaped, by the experience of the other in the analytic relationship.

What is unique about the analytic collaboration is not its intersubjective nature, but its attempt to understand and interpret its contribution to the respective participants' minds in conflict. In a sense, the intersubjective perspective is nothing more than a significant elaboration of the transference–countertransference concept.

The concept of intersubjectivity stresses the interminability of the influence of unconscious fantasy and conflict. It helps the analyst resist the seductive idea that he or she can objectively understand an experience. Instead, it suggests that the best anyone can do is be more or less able to subjectively reflect on his or her experience, while simultaneously being more or less influenced by the subjectivity of the collaborating analysand.

It is both interesting and inevitable that words and concepts acquire subjective meanings. Some of these meanings are an aspect of the seemingly interminable tendency towards revolutionary paradigm competition. In so-called classical or Freudian circles, the term *intersubjective* is associated with the terms *relational* or *interpersonal*. Thus, it is thought to reflect work that is psychotherapeutic or supportive rather than psychoanalytic. In addition, the term *intersubjective* may be associated with concepts of modes of therapeutic action that are believed to reflect fantasies of reparative cure through love.

In an important paper, Abend (1989) explored the beneficial effects on compromise formation theory of assimilation of some Kleinian elaborations of the countertransference concept. This exploration of the intersubjective concept is in pursuit of a similar goal.

I have attempted to elaborate compromise formation theory from the perspective of the postmodern contributions that have enriched our general understanding of the analytic situation, and of transference–countertransference in particular. Compromise formation theory, with its emphasis on the interminability of conflict, has always stressed the subjectivity of thought and perception in general, and of transference and countertransference in particular. In elaborating an intersubjective aspect of the theory, I stress its value for understanding the continual and reciprocal shaping and reshaping influence of the analyst and analysand on their respective transferences. This perspective stresses both the importance and limits of the analyst's personality as contributing shaping elements in the therapeutic action of psychoanalysis.

REFERENCES

Abend, S. (1989). Countertransference and psychoanalytic technique. *Psychoanalytic Quarterly, 58*: 374–395.

Abend, S., Porder, M., & Willick, M. (1983). *Borderline Patients: Psychoanalytic Perspectives*. New York: International Universities Press.

Adler, A. (1926). *The Practice and Theory of Individual Psychology*. London: Kegan Paul, Trench, Trauber.

Alexander, F. (1927). *The Psychoanalysis of the Personality*. New York and Washington: New Mental Disease Publishing, 1930.

Alexander, F. (1938). Remarks about the relation of inferiority feelings to guilt feelings. *International Journal of Psychoanalysis, 19*: 41–49.

Alexander, F. (1948). *The Fundamentals of Psychoanalysis*. New York: W. W. Norton.

American Psychiatric Association (1994). *Diagnostic and Statistical Manual of Mental Disorders*, 4th edn (*DSM-IV*), Washington, DC: American Psychiatric Press.

Arlow, J. (1969). Unconscious fantasy and disturbances of conscious experience. In: *On Psychoanalysis: Clinical Theory and Practice* (pp. 155–175). Madison, CT: International Universities Press, 1991.

Arlow, J., & Brenner, C. (1964). *Psychoanalytic Concepts and the Structural Theory*. New York: International Universities Press.

Arlow, J., & Brenner, C. (1990). The psychoanalytic process. *Psychoanalytic Quarterly, 59*: 678–692.

Aron, L. (1996). *A Meeting of Minds*. Hillsdale, NJ: Analytic Press.

Bachrach, H. (1990). The analyst's thinking and attitude at the beginning of an analysis: the influence of research data at the beginning of an analysis. In: T. Jacobs & A. Rothstein (Eds.), *On Beginning an Analysis* (pp. 3–26). Madison, CT: International Universities Press.

Bergler, E. (1961). *Curable and Incurable Neurotics*. New York: Liveright.

Berliner, B. (1940). Libido and reality in masochism. *Psychoanalytic Quarterly, 9*: 322–333.

Berliner, B. (1942). The concept of masochism. *Psychoanalytic Review, 29*: 386–400.

Berliner, B. (1947). On some psychodynamics of masochism. *Psychoanalytic Quarterly, 16*: 459–471.

Berliner, B. (1958). The role of object relations in moral masochism. *Psychoanalytic Quarterly, 27*: 358–377.

Bernstein, I. (1957). The role of narcissism in moral masochism. *Psychoanalytic Quarterly, 26*: 358–377.

Boesky, D. (1982). Acting out: a reconsideration of the concept. *International Journal of Psychoanalysis, 63*: 39–55.

Boesky, D. (1991). Applications of the theory of conflict and compromise formation to clinical phenomena: sublimation, enactment, and identification. In: A. Rothstein (Ed.), *The Moscow Lectures on Psychoanalysis* (pp. 3–26). Madison, CT: International Universities Press.

Brenner, C. (1968). Psychoanalysis and science. *Journal of the American Psychoanalytic Association, 16*: 677–696.

Brenner, C. (1974). Depression, anxiety, and a affect theory. *International Journal of Psychoanalysis, 55*: 25–32.

Brenner, C. (1975). Affects and psychic conflict. *Psychoanalytic Quarterly, 44*:189–214.

Brenner, C. (1976). *Psychoanalytic Technique and Psychic Conflict*. New York: International Universities Press.

Brenner, C. (1979a). Depression, anxiety, and affect theory. *International Journal of Psychoanalysis, 55*: 25–32.

Brenner, C. (1979b). The component of psychic conflict and its consequences in mental life. *Psychoanalytic Quarterly, 48*: 547–567.

Brenner, C. (1980). Metapsychology and psychoanalytic theory. *Psychoanalytic Quarterly, 49*: 189–214.

Brenner, C. (1982). *The Mind in Conflict*. New York: International Universities Press.

Brenner, C. (1994). The mind as conflict and compromise. *Journal of Clinical Psychoanalysis, 3*: 473–488.

Brenner, C. (1998). Beyond the ego and id revisited. *Journal of Clinical Psychoanalysis, 7*: 165–180.

Brenner, C. (2000). Observations on some aspects of current psychoanalytic theories. *Psychoanalytic Quarterly, 69*: 597–622.

Brenner, C. (2002). Conflict, compromise formation and structural theory. *Psychoanalytic Quarterly, 71*: 397–417.

Brenner, C. (2008). Aspects of psychoanalytic theory: drives, defenses and the pleasure–unpleasure principle. Presented to The New York Psychoanalytic Society, 8 April.

Broucek, F. (1982). Shame and its relationship to early narcissistic development. *International Journal of Psychoanalysis, 63*: 369–378.

Caligor, E., Stern, B. L., Hamilton, M., Maccornack, V., Wininger, L., Sneed, J., & Roose, S. P. (2009). Why we recommend analytic treatment for some patients and not for others. *Journal of the American Psychoanalytic Association, 57*: 677–694.

Cooper, A. (1977). The masochistic–narcissistic character. Unpublished manuscript.

Darwin, C. (1872). *The Expression of the Emotions in Man and Animals.* London: John Murray.

Deutsch, H. (1942). Some forms of emotional disturbance and their relation to schizophrenia. *Psychoanalytic Quarterly, 11*: 301–321.

Eidelberg, L. (1959). Humiliation and masochism. *Journal of the American Psychoanalytic Association, 7*: 274–283.

Erikson, E. (1960). *Childhood and Civilization.* New York: W. W. Norton.

Erle, J. B. (1993). On the setting of analytic fees. *Psychoanalytic Quarterly, 62*: 165–108.

Fenichel, O. (1941). *Problems of Psychoanalytic Technique.* Albany, New York: Psychoanalytic Quarterly Inc.

Freud, A. (1936). *The Ego and the Mechanisms of Defense.* New York: International Universities Press. 1946.

Freud, A. (1968). Acting out. *International Journal of Psychoanalysis, 49*: 165–170.

Freud, S. (1894). The neuro-psychoses of defence. *S.E., 3*: 45–68. London: Hogarth Press.

Freud, S. (1895a). Project for a scientific psychology. In: M. Bonaparte, A. Freud, & E. Kris (Eds.) *The Origins of Psychoanalyses: Letter to Wilhelm Fliess, Drafts, and Notes: 1887–1902* (pp. 355–445). New York: Basic Books, 1954.

Freud, S. (1895b). *Studies on Hysteria. S.E., 3:* 1–305. London: Hogarth Press.

Freud, S. (1900a). *The Interpretation of Dreams. S.E., 5.* London: Hogarth Press.

Freud, S. (1901). The psychopathology of everyday life. *S.E., 6.* London: Hogarth Press.

Freud, S. (1905a). *Three Essays on the Theory of Sexuality. S.E., 7:* 135–243. London: Hogarth Press.

Freud, S. (1905b). On psychotherapy. *S.E., 7:* 257–268. London: Hogarth Press.

Freud, S. (1909). *Notes upon a Case of Obsessional Neurosis. S.E., 10:*155–318. London: Hogarth Press.

Freud, S. (1911). Formulations on the two principles of mental functioning. *S.E., 12:* 218–226. London: Hogarth Press.

Freud, S. (1913). On beginning the treatment (Further recommendations on the technique of psycho-analysis I.) *S.E., 12:* 123–144. London: Hogarth Press.

Freud, S. (1914a). On narcissism: an introduction. *S.E., 14:* 6–109. London: Hogarth Press.

Freud, S. (1914b). Remembering, repeating and working-through. (Further recommendations on the technique of psycho-analysis II.) *S.E., 12:*147–156. London: Hogarth Press.

Freud, S. (1915a). Instincts and their vicissitudes. S.E., *14:* 117–140. London: Hogarth Press.

Freud, S. (1915b). Observations on transference love. (Further recommendations on the technique of psycho-analysis III.) *S.E., 12:* 159–171. London: Hogarth Press.

Freud, S. (1916). Some character types met with in psychoanalytic work. *S.E., 14:* 319–334. London: Hogarth Press.

Freud, S. (1917a). On transformations of instinct as exemplified in anal eroticism. *S.E., 17:* 125–133. London: Hogarth Press.

Freud, S. (1917b). Mourning and melancholia. *S.E., 14:* 243–258. London: Hogarth Press.

Freud, S. (1920). *Beyond the Pleasure Principle. S.E., 18:* 7–64. London: Hogarth Press.

Freud, S. (1923). *The Ego and the Id. S.E., 19:* 12–66. London: Hogarth Press.

Freud, S. (1924). The economic problem of masochism. *S.E., 19:* 159–170. London: Hogarth Press.

Freud, S. (1926). Inhibitions, symptoms and anxiety. *S.E., 20:* 87–156.

Freud, S. (1930). *Civilization and Its Discontents. S.E., 21*: 64–145. London: Hogarth Press.

Freud, S. (1933). *New Introductory Lectures on Psychoanalysis. S.E., 22*: 5–182. London: Hogarth Press.

Freud, S. (1937). Analysis terminable and interminable. *S.E., 23*: 216–253. London: Hogarth Press.

Freud, S. (1940). *An Outline of Psychoanalysis. S.E., 23*: 144–207. London: Hogarth Press.

Gill, M. (1994). *Psychoanalysis in Transition*. Hillsdale, NJ: Analytic Press.

Glover, E. (1955). *The Technique of Psychoanalysis*. New York: International Universities Press.

Grinker, R. (1955). Growth inertia and shame. Their therapeutic implications and dangers. *International Journal of Psychoanalysis, 36*: 242–253.

Grubrich-Simitis, I. (1986). Six letters of Sigmund Freud and Sandor Ferenczi on the interrelationship of psychoanalytic theory and technique. *International Review of Psychoanalysis, 13*: 259–277.

Grunberger, B. (1971). *Narcissism*. New York: International Universities Press.

Hamilton, M., Wininger, L., & Roose, S. P. (2009). Dropout rate of training cases: who and when. *Journal of the American Psychoanalytic Association, 57*: 695–702.

Hartmann, H. (1939). *Ego Psychology and the Problem of Adaptation*. New York: International Universities Press, 1964.

Hartmann, H. (1950). Comments on the theory of the ego. *Psychoanalytic Study of the Child, 5*: 749.

Hartmann, H., & Loewenstein, R. (1962). Notes on the superego. *Psychoanalytic Study of the Child, 17*: 42–81.

Hoffman, I. (1998). *Ritual and Spontaneity in Psychoanalytic Process: A Dialectical-Constructivist View*. Hillsdale, NJ: Analytic Press.

Jacobs, T. (1986). On countertransference enactments. *Journal of the American Psychoanalytic Association, 34*: 289–307.

Jacobs, T. (1991). *The Use of the Self*. Madison, CT: International Universities Press.

Jacobson, E. (1964). *The Self and the Object World*. New York: International Universities Press.

Kernberg, O. (1967). Borderline personality organization. *Journal of the American Psychoanalytic Association, 15*: 641–685.

Kernberg, O. (1970). Factors in the psychoanalytic treatment of narcissistic personality. *Journal of the American Psychoanalytic Association, 18*: 51–85.

Kernberg, O. (1975). *Borderline Conditions and Pathological Narcissism.* New York: Aronson.

Knight, R. (1953). Borderline states. *Bulletin of the Menninger Clinic, 17:* 142.

Kohut, H. (1959). Introspection, empathy, and psychoanalysis. An examination of the relationship between mode of observation and theory. *Journal of the American Psychoanalytic Association, 7:* 459–483.

Kohut, H. (1966). Forms and transformations of narcissism. *Journal of the American Psychoanalytic Association, 14:* 243–272.

Kohut, H. (1968). The psychoanalytic treatment of narcissistic personality disorders. *Psychoanalytic Study of the Child, 23:* 86–113. New York: International Universities Press.

Kohut, H. (1971). *The Analysis of the Self.* New York: International Universities Press.

Kohut, H. (1977). *The Restoration of the Self.* New York: International Universities Press.

Kohut, H., & Wolf, E. S. (1978). The disorders of the self and their treatment: an outline. *International Journal of Psychoanalysis, 59:* 413–425.

Kuhn, T. S. (1962). *The Structure of Scientific Revolutions.* Chicago, IL: The University of Chicago Press, 1970.

Levenson, E. A. (1983). *The Ambiguity of Change.* New York: Basic Books.

Loewenstein, R. H. (1957). A contribution to the psychoanalytic theory of masochism. *Journal of the American Psychoanalytic Association, 5:* 197–234.

Modell, A. H. (1988). On the protection and safety of the therapeutic setting. In: A. Rothstein (Ed.), *How Does Treatment Help?* (pp. 95–104). Madison, CT: International Universities Press.

Morrison, A. (1984). Working with shame in psychoanalytic treatment. *Journal of the American Psychoanalytic Association, 32:* 479–505.

Olinick, S. (1964). The negative therapeutic reaction. *International Journal of Psychoanalysis, 45:* 540–548.

Piers, G., & Singer, M. (1953). *Shame and Guilt.* New York: W. W. Norton, 1971.

Rado, S. (1933). Fear of castration in women. *Psychoanalytic Quarterly, 2:* 425–475.

Renik, O. (1993). Analytic interaction: conceptualizing technique in light of the analyst's irreducible subjectivity. *Psychoanalytic Quarterly, 62:* 553–571.

Robbins, M. (1983). Toward a new mind model for the primitive personalities. *International Journal of Psychoanalysis, 64:* 127–148.

Rothstein, A. (1977). The ego attitude of entitlement. *International Review of Psychoanalysis*, 4: 409–417.

Rothstein, A. (1979a). Oedipal conflicts in narcissistic personality disorders. *International Journal of Psychoanalysis*, 60: 189–199.

Rothstein, A. (1979b). An exploration of the diagnostic term narcissistic personality disorder. *Journal of the American Psychoanalytic Association*, 27: 893–912.

Rothstein, A. (1980). *The Narcissistic Pursuit of Perfection*. New York: International Universities Press.

Rothstein, A. (1983). *The Structural Hypothesis: An Evolutionary Perspective*. New York: International Universities Press.

Rothstein, A. (1984). Fear of humiliation. *Journal of the American Psychoanalytic Association*, 32: 99–116.

Rothstein, A. (1988). The representation world as a substructure of the ego. *Journal of the American Psychoanalytic Association*, 36(Suppl.): 191–208.

Rothstein, A. (1990). On beginning with a reluctant patient. In: J. Jacobs & A. Rothstein (Eds.), *On Beginning an Analysis* (pp. 153–162). Madison, CT: International Universities Press.

Rothstein, A. (1991). On some relationships between fantasies of perfection and the calamities of childhood. *International Journal of Psychoanalysis*, 72: 313–323.

Rothstein, A. (1994). Shame and the superego: clinical and theoretical considerations. *Psychoanalytic Study of the Child*, 49: 263–277.

Rothstein, A. (1998). *Psychoanalytic Technique and the Creations of Analytic Patients*, 2nd edn. Madison, CT: International Universities Press.

Rothstein, A. (2008). Discussion of Charles Brenner's aspects of psychoanalytic theory: drives, defenses and the pleasure–unpleasure principle. Presented to *The New York Psychoanalytic Society*, 8 April 2008.

Schafer, R. (1968). *Aspects of Internalization*. New York: International Universities Press.

Schafer, R. (1976). *A New Language for Psychoanalysis*. New York: International Universities Press.

Shengold, L. (1994). Envy and malignant masochism. *Psychoanalytic Quarterly*, 63: 615–640.

Socarides, C. W. (1958). The function of moral masochism: with special reference to the defense process. *International Journal of Psychoanalysis*, 39: 587–597.

Stein, M. H. (1956). Report of the panel on the problem of masochism in the theory and technique of psychoanalysis. *Journal of the American Psychoanalytic Association, 4*: 526–538.

Stein, M. H. (1973). Acting out as a character trait. Its relation to the transference. *Psychoanalytic Study of the Child, 28*: 347–364.

Stern, A. (1938). Psychoanalytic investigation of and therapy in the borderline groups of neuroses. *Psychoanalytic Quarterly, 7*: 467–489.

Stolorow, R. (1995). An intersubjective view of self psychology. *Psychoanalytic Dialogues, 5*: 393–400.

Stone, L. (1954). The widening scope of indications for psychoanalysis. *Journal of the American Psychoanalytic Association, 2*: 567–594.

Valenstein, A. S. (1973). On attachments to painful feelings and the negative therapeutic reaction. *Psychoanalytic Study of the Child, 28*: 365–392.

Varnedoe, K. (1990). *A Fine Disregard: What Makes Modern Art Modern.* New York: Harry N. Abrams.

Willick, M. (1993). The deficit syndrome in psychoanalysis: psychoanalytic and neurobiological perspectives. *Journal of the American Psychoanalytic Association, 41*: 1135–1157.

Yorke, C., Balogh, T., Cohen, P., Davids, J., Gavshon, A., McCutcheon, M., McLean, D., Miller, J., & Syzdio, J. (1990). The development and functioning of the sense of shame. *Psychoanalytic Study of the Child, 45*: 377–409.

INDEX